"Helpful, practical, and easy to read—this was my first response to this book. Many readers will find their questions answered in a supportive and encouraging manner. It's a hopeful resource designed to bring hope."

—**H. Norman Wright**, Grief and Certified Trauma Specialist

"It's tough to believe that a subject so unwieldy can be made so readable, but this book pulls it off. *Seeing in the Dark* is an important resource on depression: candid, knowledgeable, understanding, and even engrossing. Gary Kinnaman and Dr. Richard Jacobs—a pastor and a doctor—are ideal sources of wisdom on this puzzling topic, and they approach the issue with real knowledge, real insight, and real compassion. We've needed a work like this for a long time."

—**Ted Haggard**, President of National Association of Evangelicals and
    Senior Pastor, New Life Church

"There is grace all over this book. It breathes hope, understanding, and wisdom. I will give copies to family members, friends, and co-workers. I am certain it will help all who read it."

—**Floyd McClung**, Director, All Nations

"What I love about *Seeing in the Dark* is that it encapsulates everything I have long admired about Pastor Gary Kinnaman (traits that are equally evident in his writing partner, Dr. Richard Jacobs). It deals forthrightly with a vital topic the church is afraid to handle and does so with heaping doses of grace, humor, and just plain common sense. Well-written and well-researched, this book is a gift to the body of Christ that will have far-reaching impact.

"If you or someone you know struggles with depression, you'll discover invaluable insight and practical suggestions for treating this often misunderstood condition. Best of all, there is now no condemnation for those struggling with depression."

—**Donna Partow**, Author, *Becoming the Woman I Want to Be*

"Genuinely spiritual people have views of depression that run the whole gamut, from 'Christians should never be depressed' to 'just take a pill and get over it.' *Seeing in the Dark* gives all of us hopeful, realistic, and sane advice for getting help ourselves and for relating better to friends and family who battle depression. Gary and Richard's book helps break the power of guilt, fear, and isolation. They help us stop judging and being judged regarding depression."

—**Todd Hunter**, National Director, Alpha USA

Books by
Gary Kinnaman

And Signs Shall Follow
Angels: Dark and Light
Beginner's Guide to Praise and Worship
Dumb Things Smart Christians Believe
Experiencing the Power of the Cross
Leaders That Last (with Alfred Ells)
Learning to Love the One You Marry
My Companion Through Grief
The Spirit-Filled Life Study Bible: Acts
Winning Your Spiritual Battles

getting the facts on **depression**
& finding hope again

seeing in the dark

Gary Kinnaman
Richard Jacobs, MD

BETHANYHOUSE
MINNEAPOLIS, MINNESOTA

Published by Bethany House Publishers
11400 Hampshire Avenue South
Bloomington, Minnesota 55438

Bethany House Publishers is a division of
Baker Publishing Group, Grand Rapids, Michigan.

Printed in the United States of America

ISBN-13: 978-0-7642-0199-8
ISBN-10: 0-7642-0199-9

Library of Congress Cataloging-in-Publication Data

Kinnaman, Gary.
 Seeing in the dark : getting the facts on depression and finding hope again / Gary Kinnaman and Richard Jacobs.
  p. cm.
 Summary: "A first-person account of depression from a pastor who experiences depression and a medical doctor whose wife deals with clinical depression. Discusses symptoms, physiological, psychological, and spiritual aspects of depression along with misconceptions and treatment options"—Provided by publisher.
 Includes index.
 ISBN 0-7642-0199-9 (pbk.)
 1. Depression, Mental 2. Kinnaman, Gary. I. Jacobs, Richard (Richard D.) II. Title.
 RC537.K534   2006
 616.85'27—dc22   2006013731

To those who are close to me
who have suffered with depression.
And to my dear wife, Marilyn, my kids, and close friends
who have loved and encouraged me
because of, and in spite of, who I am.
   —Gary Kinnaman

To Sue,
my best friend, partner, and wife for over thirty-three years.
"Many women do noble things, but you surpass them all."
   —PROVERBS 31:29

and to my mom and dad, Marcia and Rich,
whose sacrifice and love led me to Christ.
   —Richard Jacobs, MD

about the authors

GARY KINNAMAN is senior pastor of the 6,000 member Word of Grace Church near Phoenix. He is a graduate of Biola University (BA), Arizona State University (MA), Fuller Theological Seminary (MA in Theology), Western Conservative Baptist Seminary (DMin). Gary has planted several other churches in Arizona, is a popular conference speaker, and is the founder of an emerging, national movement of covenant groups for pastors (Pastors in Covenant). Gary and his wife, Marilyn, who make their home in Mesa, Arizona, have three adult children and five grandchildren.

RICHARD JACOBS, MD, is the chief medical officer and vice-president of medical operations for a large health plan in Arizona. His avocation is astronomy, and his astrophotographs have been published in magazines worldwide. Active in Crossroads Church of the Nazarene, Rich teaches adult Sunday school and serves on the church board. He and his wife, Sue, have two adult children and live in the Phoenix area.

acknowledgments

Many thanks to the many people who make a book like this a reality . . .

- Kyle, thanks for inviting me to write for Bethany House.

- Rich, for your extraordinary gifts, which have made this an extraordinary book.

- Sue, for letting your husband (and me) tell your story.

- Jeanne, thanks for making the manuscript so much better.

- Sherry, for your excellent work as my personal assistant.

- Penny Jo, thanks for your friendship and your professional help retyping portions of the manuscript and for the daunting task of preparing an index.

- The Reverends Keith, Cal, Mark D., Mark F., Phil, Alan, and Scott (my covenant group), for your wisdom, friendship, and encouragement over the last number of years.

- Gary, Al, Harold, Daryl, Dan, Mark B., and Len, my very good friends and colleagues, thanks for everything you mean to me.

—Gary Kinnaman

Thanks to ...

- Pastor Gary Kinnaman—for asking me to be a part of this book and for all that you've taught me in the process of writing it.

- Pastor Mark Fuller—for introducing me to Gary and for having the confidence that I would be able to make a meaningful contribution to this project.

- Sue, Sal R., and Jen—for reading and critiquing my first drafts.

- Bethany House Publishers—for all their help, and for caring enough about those who suffer with depression to sponsor this book.

—Richard Jacobs, MD

contents

Have you ever heard of a race called the Global Challenge? It's not a super-marathon that you run on land. Actually, it's a sailing race—*which, believe it or not, has a great deal to do with depression*—so please read on.

It seems that for hundreds of years sailors have been perfectly content to sail—and even race—on the ocean using the prevailing winds and ocean currents to speed them along. But that's not what the Global Challenge does. This race isn't a sprint. It is a race that circumnavigates the entire earth. And if a round-the-world race isn't challenging enough, it's all done by sailing nonstop—*backward!* Instead of sailing in an ever-easterly direction, the entire race goes *opposite* the prevailing winds and currents.

During this race, there are times when the seventy-two-foot sailing ships will face seventy-mile-per-hour winds and fifty-foot waves breaking over the bows, sending icy cold water crashing over anyone on deck. Then just a few weeks later, those same ships can face stifling heat and winds so still that it seems like no one on board will ever reach the horizon.

When I first read about the Global Challenge, held once every four years, I thought of what a beautiful picture that was of the daily challenge many men and women face. The crews manning the ships that run the Global Challenge are all volunteers. Depression presses people on deck, against their wishes, for a journey that seems like it will never end. And like the challenges those sailors face voluntarily, depression can leave us feeling like we're without choices, as numb inside as if we've been hit with a sheet of arctic water. Depression can also turn around and leave us feeling stuck in a place where it seems there isn't a breath of wind for change, and where *minutes* can seem like a never-ending eternity with no hope in sight or confidence that the goals we once had will ever be reached.

What steers those ships through such tremendous challenges are their captains, who have years of sailing wisdom. This book has two such captains who are ready to invest their lives and wisdom into your life-journey. Gary Kinnaman, in his role as pastor, has spent decades working with people struggling with depression, and Dr. Richard Jacobs has spent years working to defeat depression in his role as physician. Together they make the perfect team that you or a loved one needs to reach safe harbor. And there's more.

In this book, you'll find firsthand stories, keen biblical insights, and the most current, helpful research and tools to help you "see in the dark." For when the waves are high or the winds are still, it's even worse at night. What these two godly men do is provide God's light to the most challenging life situations.

You'll love the way these two authors team up to educate, encourage, and motivate you to face the realities before you with words that really can help. They have both looked depression eye to eye in the lives of loved ones and hundreds of people just like you and me—and have seen convincing proof that there's hope and help for each of us. So even if the challenge before you seems as big as the Global Challenge, you've picked up the right book to help you tack and steer and set the sails in your life to get you headed in the right direction.

And one more thought for you, the reader. If you're new to Scripture, keep in mind that several times the Lord brought His people safely through the storm and dark waters. (Think of Noah and the shipwrecked apostle Paul as two examples.) In the book of Acts we read, "And so it happened that they were all safely brought to land" (27:44). That same God who brought Paul and those ship-wrecked with him through the storm can bring you safely to shore as well. So turn the page and you'll see how that even when times are the darkest, most challenging, and most confusing there really is a way to see in the dark.

—John Trent, PhD
Author of *The Blessing* and *The 2 Degree Difference*
President, The Center for StrongFamilies, Scottsdale, Arizona

chapter 1

The Valley of the Shadow:

Rich and Sue's Journey Through the Darkness

*In my anguish I cried to the Lord, and he answered
by setting me free.*
—Psalm 118:5

Life can only be understood backwards; but
it must be lived forwards.
—Søren Kierkegaard

"I want a divorce!"

I couldn't believe my ears. Sue and I (Rich) had just had one of
our rare spats. I can't even remember what we were fighting about.
Neither can she, but our trivial argument led to Sue's demand for a
divorce. I was dumbfounded and afraid. We were both Christians,
and neither of us believed in divorce. I thought we were happily
married. Yet something was deeply wrong, and I didn't have a clue
what it was.

Sue and I were teenage sweethearts. I was only seventeen when
I fell madly in love with this petite, blue-eyed beauty. She was six-
teen and, in the estimation of her father, far too young to be going
steady with the likes of me. Still, we dated no one else until we
became engaged and married five years later.

Sue earned her RN degree and graduated from nursing school

after our first year of marriage. I had only completed my first year of medical school. Three years later our daughter, Jenny, was born. By this time I was in the middle of my internship, working one hundred hours per week. The crushing work load of my medical residency program continued another two years, until our son, Steven, was born. Then it was time for us to repay the U.S. Navy for the scholarship that financed most of my medical-school education.

The Navy packed us off to Guam, an island in the middle of the Pacific Ocean, over seven thousand miles from home, family, and friends. Sue was having to mother two toddlers, one still in diapers. I was facing the sobering reality that I was now a "real doctor" and had to take care of people without the support and advice of professors or key specialists. The last several years had been so very difficult for us, and it all came to a head when we were in Guam. The stress and loneliness we experienced there nearly ended our marriage.

By God's grace we did not get a divorce. In time we found a church, made other friends, and began attending a Bible fellowship in our neighborhood. Life seemed to return to normal. What we didn't know at the time, and what we only now realize in retrospect, is that Sue had been clinically depressed during most of our first year on the island.

Depression Is Creepy

It's astounding to me that two people with as much medical education and training as Sue and I had could have missed this diagnosis. But that's the way it is with depression: It sneaks up on you. It begins so slowly and insidiously in its victims that the symptoms of depression can be mistaken for other problems. R. W. Shepherd wrote, "If depression is creeping up and must be faced, learn something about the nature of the beast; you may escape without a mauling."[1] About five to seven percent of the population has serious clinical depression at any given time.[2] Almost a quarter of the patients who see their family doctor have major depressive symptoms.[3] Depression is fairly common. Nonetheless, about half of these patients go completely undiagnosed by anyone.[4]

Sue was a registered nurse, and she didn't realize she was depressed. All she knew was that she felt terrible and was very unhappy. Being married to a physician who also did not suspect that his wife was clinically depressed didn't help either. She had many of the common symptoms, but I always found some other explanation for them. I just didn't put all the pieces together.

She was losing weight, taking frequent naps during the day, and having trouble sleeping at night. Uncharacteristically irritable, she broke into tears at the slightest provocation. I often wondered, *Is it that time of month?* Sue was keeping the house clean and taking care of the kids, but she was not pursuing any of her other usual interests. Much later, I learned that Sue even experienced fleeting thoughts of suicide.

When you put all of Sue's symptoms together, the unmistakable picture of depression emerges. A number of major stressors in life can cause a depressive episode in vulnerable people.[5] We certainly had those, given all our life changes at that time. Furthermore, Sue had a family history of depression and alcoholism. Those warning signs should have alerted us to her condition.[6] Many people with depression treat their pain with drugs or alcohol, and females have a higher risk for depression than males.[7]

Sue had dark moods, weight loss, insomnia at night and sleepiness during the day, loss of energy, a lack of interest in hobbies, and thoughts of suicide. These are the classic symptoms of major depression,[8] and Sue was a poster child. We both thought, though, that depression was something that happened to others—not us. That's another reason why many folks don't recognize they have depression: They never consider that it could happen to them!

What's to Love About Depressed People?

Over the last thirty years of practicing medicine, I've come to admire the resilience and strength of people who suffer from depression. A Japanese proverb teaches us: *Fall seven times, stand up eight.* My wife has been a wonderful example of this. Sue never gave up being a good wife and mother. She cared for the kids, prepared great meals, and made our house a home. Inside, though, she wanted to shrivel up and die.

Most people with clinical depression suffer quietly from their condition while carrying on with life the best they can. That's what Sue did. We now know her depression in Guam was not her first encounter with emotional darkness; depression paid her a visit during her freshman year at the University of Missouri, seven years earlier. Looking back, we now realize all the same symptoms were present, but Sue applied herself in her studies and did her best to get on with life. She just sucked it up and gutted it out for about a year through each of her first two bouts with depression. I, on the other hand, lie around, grouse, and feel sorry for myself when I get a common cold. Somehow Sue survived her bouts with depression without any meaningful treatment. She didn't even know she was depressed!

It's a myth that people with depression are somehow less resilient than other human beings, or are fundamentally dysfunctional or lazy. Sue's depression was a real physical illness. Fortunately, her first two attacks were relatively mild episodes of the disease, but all that changed in the mid-1990s.

Sue seemed to be back to "normal," and life was great. By this time we had relocated to Arizona and were loving it. We settled into an excellent church. Our kids were doing great. I was well established in my new practice and making a good living. We were happily married. We had friends, and many of our family members visited us from out of town every winter. Everyone was healthy, happy, and prospering. Everyone, that is, except Sue.

For no good reason Sue began her third, and most severe, episode of depression in 1992. This was the attack of the disease that finally awakened us to her true condition. Many believe severe depression has to have some significant cause. Indeed, the tragic loss of a loved one can bring on depression, but for Sue, everything in her life at the time was positive and upbeat—except for the way she felt inside. It mystified us. It even made me angry. Sue and I were trained, experienced medical professionals . . . how could depression hit us? We thought you had to have a *good reason* to be depressed, but we discovered that

Depression is not an emotional problem.

Does that statement surprise you? Yes, depression has prominent emotional symptoms. It is not sadness, although people with depression are sad. Simple sadness and grief are caused by loss or tragedy, and although loss or tragedy can trigger depression, depression is much more than sadness. Like all medical conditions, depression has physical, mental, emotional, and spiritual effects. When an individual becomes ill the *whole person* suffers. Depression, like asthma and diabetes, doesn't need any "reason" to occur—it just does. Depression is an illness.

My wife's most recent bout began as simple fatigue and a loss of energy, but it became progressively worse. Her loss of energy gradually became so significant that she was spending most of the day in bed while I was away at work. Insomnia began to interrupt her normal patterns of sleep. She had trouble falling asleep at night and, unable to resume sleep, would often awaken early in the morning. Sue had no appetite, and she began to lose weight.

This time she had trouble keeping up with her household chores. She didn't even have the energy to be irritable. Then the emotional symptoms of her illness began to set in. Bouts of crying seemed to come from nowhere. Constantly sad, Sue found less and less pleasure in life. Eventually her depression became so severe she had difficulty concentrating, thinking, even expressing herself. She abandoned her special interests and hobbies, and her libido vanished.

Ironically, when she needed God the most, a spiritual death set in. She no longer believed God could love her. She didn't believe she was worthy of being loved by anyone. Haunted by feelings and thoughts of worthlessness, Sue developed a preoccupation with death and dying. Once again, she toyed with thoughts of suicide. She felt so miserable that she welcomed the end of her life.

Sue's dim-witted doctor/husband should have been able to identify her illness, but we consulted an objective, outside physician for help. She informed us that Sue, indeed, had a serious case of depression, for which she prescribed Sertraline (Zoloft). Sertraline belongs to a class of antidepressant medications called "Serotonin Re-uptake Inhibitors," or SRI for short. SRIs repair the chemical imbalance in the brain that can cause depression.[9] Research indicates that certain people at risk for depression may use up the chemical messengers in their brains, called neurotransmitters, faster than they make them. *People who do not suffer from depression are free from this metabolic problem.* That makes it difficult for them to understand why someone who is depressed can't just pray their way out of it.

These chemical messengers connect one part of our brain to another so that thoughts and emotions can occur normally. One of these chemical messengers is serotonin.[10] A person experiences depression when brain serotonin levels become lower than normal. Low brain serotonin levels cause fatigue, sadness, and difficulty concentrating. Other chemical messengers can be depleted in depression too, but SRIs help restore them to normal levels. For Sue and me, our hope was that Sertraline would help her recover from depression by correcting the chemistry in her brain.

It's a myth that antidepressant medications like SRIs are addicting, like narcotics. Other people believe that antidepressants are "uppers," like methamphetamine or cocaine. Nothing could be further from the truth. Certainly, antidepressants can have unwelcome side effects, like any medication, but most of these side effects greatly diminish or vanish with time.

People with depression are frequently reluctant to take medication for three good reasons: fear, shame, and the side effects of the treatment. During the first week of treatment, for example, Sue experienced both the symptoms of her depression *and* the side effects of the medicine, including some diarrhea. We joked that the medication was literally getting things moving again for Sue! Maintaining symptoms and having side effects is typical for patients first treated for depression, and it's no fun. Often, though, medication is their best hope for a rapid recovery from their illness. (Chapter 6 will explore in more detail the role of medication in treating depression.)

Paradoxically, for some severely depressed patients and for adolescents, the risk of suicide may actually increase during the first week or so of treatment with medication.[11] No one knows why. One theory is that severely depressed patients simply don't have the energy or initiative to carry out their suicidal ideas. The early stages of recovery from medication treatment may restore enough energy to the patient to take their own life before the pain and misery of the depression has been fully remedied. In any event, it is vital that patients and the families of patients be alerted to this danger so that appropriate precautions can be taken.

After about ten days of medication my wife began to feel better. Her sadness and feelings of worthlessness lessened. She had more energy. Her sleep patterns began to normalize. Although her doctors had to adjust the dosage of her medication twice, we were grateful that the first medication prescribed for her seemed to be working. Sometimes a patient may have to try several different drugs before finding the right one, while other patients need more than one medication to halt their depression. In our case, after three months of treatment, Sue seemed to have returned to normal again.

Living the Truth

Sue has been free from depression for over ten years now, but she hasn't been free from her medication. Neither of us liked the idea of her remaining on her antidepressant longterm. As we've already seen, one of the myths most of us believe is that there is something inherently wrong with taking medication for depression. Even after that hurdle is successfully overcome, just around the curve of the track is another: "You feel better now. You don't need to *keep* taking medication." In most cases, people who take medication for depression will likely have to *continue* to take it. Some people can come off their medication, but no one should do so without a consultation with their doctor.

As medical pros, Sue and I both knew that people who have had two episodes of major depression have over an 80 percent chance of suffering from it off and on for the rest of their lives. We also knew that untreated depression leads to significant adverse structural changes in the brain.[12] Still, we made several attempts to wean Sue from her medication, thinking that would enable her to discontinue using it altogether. But the depression always came back.

There was a pattern to the way Sue's depression would return: First she would experience fatigue and mild sadness, followed by a disruption of her normal sleep. This seemed to cause her appetite to fail, which of course led to weight loss. Yet as Sue learned how to "resist the devil" (more on this in chapter 6), she had no more thoughts of worthlessness or suicidal ideas.

After weaning and discontinuing my wife's medication, we remained vigilant for the first sign of the disease's return. I instructed her to put a little "frowny face"— 🙁 —on the calendar each day she felt sad. After a couple of months without her medication, frowny faces appeared on the calendar here and there. After a while, though, frowny faces popped up in short rows. Within about six weeks frowny faces scowled on every day of the week. This allowed us to recognize the reemergence of the disease. We strongly recommend this for anyone considering discontinuing their medication.

> Every good and perfect gift is from above, coming down from the Father of the heavenly lights (James 1:17).

We believe that SRIs are a gift from the Lord. Although depression has been Sue's thorn in the flesh, God has also used it to strengthen and bless both of us spiritually. Our prayer is that her story will liberate thousands of others from the slavery of soul darkness. Sue's story, we believe, will be significantly instrumental in demythologizing depression.

In the next chapter we'll hear from someone else who has been down that road—my coauthor, Gary Kinnaman. Some readers might be surprised to hear that he is a Christian pastor.

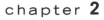

chapter 2

"Depressed Christian" Is Not an Oxymoron:

Confronting Myths About Depression

I've never thought of my characters as being sad. On the contrary, they are full of life. They didn't choose tragedy. Tragedy chose them.

— JULIETTE BINOCHE, FRENCH ACTRESS

I have depression, but first I want to tell you a story.

Something snapped.

I (Gary) knew where I was and what I was doing, but it was surreal. For a moment, I really thought I was dreaming.

A similiar thing happened to a good friend of mine, a plumber. Buff was under a customer's sink and, blink, he didn't have a clue where he was or why he was there. Somehow he had the presence of mind to grab his cell phone and call his wife. She appealed to him anxiously, *"Don't go anywhere.* I will find you and come and get you." She did, and within a couple of hours Buff was fine.

Doctors call it a TIA, a Transient Ischemic Attack—a "minor" stroke. It's a moment when blood fails to reach some tiny crevice in your head and, deprived of oxygen, a part of the brain short-circuits.[1]

Buff's episode was private, but mine was in front of a thousand people. Late last spring, I was speaking in our early Sunday service. Halfway through my talk—*wham*—I went blank. Brain numb, I looked down at my notes, the ones I had been using for the last fifteen minutes or so, and they made absolutely no sense to me. I was convinced I had picked up the wrong folder on the way to church.

I've had speaker's block, and I've lost my train of thought. I've even had notes that didn't make sense! But never this. I was convinced I was looking at the wrong sermon outline. For a moment everybody thought it was a stunt because I'm often unpredictable in making a point. But when I called my service director up to the platform to have a look at my notes and argued with her, people started to realize something was terribly wrong. I even read aloud the sermon title: "Don't bet your life on what you don't know," and announced to the whole congregation, "These are the *wrong* notes!"

As I staggered down from the platform in confusion and dismay, a physician's assistant in the congregation walked quickly to the front of the church, looked deeply into my glassy eyes, and stated firmly, "I think you've had a TIA. You need to get medical attention immediately."

Something Crazy in My Head

Knowing something crazy was happening in my head, I returned to the platform briefly, introduced myself as Greg Dille (he's our worship leader . . . I can never resist an opportunity to get a laugh), and told our congregation that I needed to be taken to the hospital. By the time I reached the foyer paramedics were arriving, and to the dismay of people arriving for the next service, there was Pastor Gary being loaded into an ambulance!

The rear doors were open, and I could see a woman looking in, with eyes affright and a hand over her mouth. She and others could see me lying there in the emergency vehicle *reading my sermon notes*! I was still trying to figure out what had happened and find my way back to reality.

I waved at her and shouted, "God really moved!"

I spent two days in the hospital for multiple tests. The doctors found nothing. One of them told me to go home and take an aspirin a day. Laughing, I replied, "You went to medical school? I just had thousands of dollars worth of tests, and you're telling me to go home and take an aspirin?"

He laughed too and admitted, "These kinds of episodes are elusive."[2] In a follow-up appointment with my family doctor, when I described the incident, he used the word "weird." He didn't even include the term "TIA" in his official report. He called it an "episode of global amnesia," but he assured me that I had little to worry about. I am encouraged by my complete recovery.

The important people in my life—my family, friends, and colleagues—were delighted too. But because of where it happened—in the house of God with a thousand people staring at my foggy face on our giant projection screen—things did not die down as quickly as we hoped. I heard days later that the word on the street was that I had either experienced a stroke or a heart attack and had *passed out on the platform* (none of which was true). It was even said by someone that I had had an episode of Tourette's syndrome and had to be carried, cursing, out of the church! To make matters worse, well-meaning but misinformed people had "messages from God" for me, advice from their mother-in-law in New Jersey, and "vital" information from the Internet to help me understand what *really* happened that fateful Sunday morning, and what I should do about it.

Myths.

Sometimes advice from others just makes you laugh. (Later, of course, because you wouldn't want to laugh *at* them.) Other times their advice is hurtful, even devastating, even though the last thing most people want to do is cause pain to someone else.

D-Myths

Fortunately, my "episode" was fleeting, and looking back, I have to smile when I remember my much-more-than-a-senior moment. But people who suffer with depression, like me, can't just laugh and let it go. Not only do they have to live at times feeling deep darkness in their soul, but what they *think* about their condition—reinforced by what other well-meaning people think they should think—complicates the problem and increases their pain. It's like the Old Testament account of Job. His friends tried really hard to give him good advice—like the well-meaning people in my church prescribed "cures" for my brain cramp—but missed the mark because they didn't or couldn't understand the deeper issues.

What people commonly think about depression is a witch's brew of everything from wrong ideas about God and the Bible to what Tom Cruise had to say about Brooke Shields' severe postpartum depression: "There is no such thing as a chemical imbalance, and depression can be cured with vitamins and exercise."[3] People have crazy ideas about why people experience mental problems, and if you pay attention to everything you hear, it may make you even more depressed! These myths pertaining specifically to depression (D-myths) are deeply entrenched in the minds of many people, even those who suffer from depression! We have listed the most common ones in Appendix A at the back of the book.

Unless you've experienced depression, or you are a trained professional, you may not understand what it is or how to treat it.

That's why we are writing this book. I (Gary) have struggled with low-grade chronic depression (the technical term is dysthymia) for most of my life. For years I've wanted to tell my story because of all the misunderstanding about depression, especially in the Christian community. I am living proof (one of the many) that Christians can and do suffer from depression! It's time to acknowledge this fact and learn how we can deal with it in the most constructive way possible.

Not long ago a friend of mine in full-time ministry shared with me about his serious depression over losing a child. He had always suffered with some elements of depression in his life, but his loss pushed him over the edge. I suggested he speak to his doctor about the possibility of taking medication, and I'll never forget his response. He was really surprised—and relieved—that I would suggest this to him. *Surprised* because, for so many Christians, the idea of taking medication for depression is, well, unchristian. And *relieved* because someone he really respected encouraged him to get medical attention. This gave him hope for change.

I asked, "If you have a bad headache, do you take an Advil?"

"Of course," he said.

"Does that make you feel guilty? Does taking an Advil for a headache somehow mean you're a bad person, or you don't have faith in God?"

"Of course not!" he replied.

"Okay, then, why does taking meds for depression make you feel ashamed in some way?" I added.

I let him know matter-of-factly that I had taken medication for depression and it really helped me. I reminded him about what he already knew: Even though wholeness in life involves so many other important elements, like spiritual disciplines, exercise, proper diet, and healthy sleep patterns, depression can *fundamentally* be a physiological problem. In other words, it can signal trouble in the brain. This is most often the case with people who suffer with major depression, the kind that's not always a result of a particular difficulty or loss in life. It's the kind of depression that just hangs over you like the early summer clouds and fog over San Diego.

My friend is doing much better! He's grateful I suggested he consider medication. He discovered that depression is a comprehensive problem. While treatment most certainly must include a discussion of God and spirituality, it's a D-myth that *people who are close to God shouldn't have a problem with depression.* Another common D-myth is that *people who are depressed should just "shake it off and cheer up."*

Maybe we could call depression a cognitive/emotional TIA. It's not that, medically speaking. But depression is something in the brain gone wrong, making you feel so blue. You read the Bible, pray, try to think positive thoughts, and the gray clouds break. Slightly. But they won't go away. Or maybe they even get darker.

I have a hunch that, if he were living today, my dear great-grandfather would have been diagnosed with clinical depression. Immigrating to the United States from Germany in the late 1800s, he began his adult life as an ordained Lutheran pastor. A brilliant and tender man, he couldn't overcome the feelings of deep darkness inside him. Not unlike Martin Luther himself, my great-grandfather, though he preached grace, couldn't seem to receive it for himself. Reading the Bible actually made him feel worse about himself, so he left the ministry to become a farmer.

Depressed Christians

"Depressed Christian" *isn't* an oxymoron, although many believers think so. When I've confessed to my congregation that I wrestle with depression, many of them are troubled. (Not depressed, of course, because Christians can't be that!) While some studies have shown that religious people are generally less depressed than those who are not religious, nevertheless, many good Christians are "cast down." Very often, they are the ones who are in full-time Christian work.

Years ago, I was speaking at a Youth With a Mission (YWAM) adult discipleship school . . . in Hawaii! The weather was fantastic, and I had received some really good news from someone on my church staff back home—for the first time ever our attendance had topped two thousand. Yet I was feeling depressed! Why? There was no good reason. It was—and is—just in me.

I shared that with the class. I couldn't tell you what the exact context was; I've just always been pretty open about my personal struggles in life, and my personal pain illustrated something I was teaching. I didn't go into the depths of my darkness. I just talked about it briefly and sincerely. At the end of the week, the class leaders asked the students to give me feedback on my teaching.

A teary-eyed woman stood up and said, "The highlight for me was when you told us you were depressed. I can't tell you how much that meant to me, to hear a Christian leader speaking honestly about what was going on in his soul. I've suffered silently for so long," she confessed. "You haven't given me an excuse to be depressed, but you've affirmed me in my pain. I'm so encouraged to know I am not alone."

That's what she got out of my fifteen hours of lectures!

A Silent Epidemic

Did you know that 80 percent of pastors in the United States are discouraged or dealing with depression, and the numbers are similar for their spouses?[4] E. Glenn Wagner, who had to leave local church ministry because of debilitating depression, calls it a "stealth epidemic." He writes, "The stealth nature of depression among pastors makes it difficult to identify and treat. . . . Even more difficult is the fact that once a pastor is diagnosed with depression, many churches are not safe places in which they may find support and healing. Depression among pastors is still a dirty secret that many churches don't wish to disclose, address, and cure."[5]

My good friend Phil Toole is a successful pastor of a great church in north Scottsdale, a suburb of Phoenix, Arizona.[6] Phil had a serious bout with personal darkness, calling it a journey *with* depression. Following is his story, told in his own words.

> After growing up in a strong Christian home and then serving in ministry for about fifteen years, I was two or three years into planting a new church when I begin to notice that something was definitely wrong inside of me. In the fervor and chaos of planting a new church and having it start well, I was surprised it didn't give me a greater sense of personal satisfaction. I found myself strangely lacking the joy and peace I thought I should have experienced.
>
> In fact, it became more and more difficult for me to get out of bed to face the day, and my wife would tell you I was becoming increasingly irritable. Even little things harassed me. One Sunday, after packing up all the equipment we needed for our temporary church location, I remember leaving the place feeling as empty as the vacant room. As I drove away, alone in my vehicle, I remember saying out loud, "If everyone else left today feeling like me, they won't be back. I am no better for having been here." It's the irony of ministry: Other people were blessed, but I was dying inside.
>
> My upbringing in a very strong Christian family seemed to make my problem worse. I presumed that whatever was wrong in me was a sign of a spiritual weakness. So if I just prayed more, read my Bible more, memorized more Scripture—or maybe did some fasting—I'd get better for sure. But none of that was helping, although my spiritual life may have been keeping me from sinking deeper.

During that time two friends of mine, one a clinical psychologist and the other a sports psychiatrist, thought I was suffering from some of the typical symptoms of depression. After hearing me talk about what I was experiencing, they *both* felt I should see my doctor and spend time with a professional counselor who wasn't a close friend. To my dismay, they suggested I might need medication!

I resisted the medication idea because of my background. I believed I should be able to overcome my problem spiritually—that God would heal me. I still believe that! I believe God can heal anything He wills, but I began to understand that depression had a physiological dimension. Before my own bout with depression I dismissed it as an emotional or mental problem. This was reinforced by people I had seen who had been medicated for depression. You know, they were people who were kind of out of it, with glazed eyes and slurred speech. It seemed like the medication just made them worse.[7] *I didn't want any of that!*

The more I learned about the body's chemical balances, however, the more I began to see that in many cases, depression can be a physiological condition, a literal problem with the brain that affects what you feel and think. So with some reluctance, I gave in to my doctor's advice and began taking an antidepressant. At first I didn't think much about it. When I went back for my first follow-up appointment, he asked how I thought the meds were working. I told him that I didn't think they were working because I felt pretty normal. When he pressed me about what I meant by normal, I realized "normal" wasn't ecstasy. I guess I sort of thought the meds would make me feel really great, like some kind of upper. Yet the oppressively dark feelings I had been battling were gone.

My doc told me, "The way you know the meds are working is *you just feel normal.* You realize you are coping better with life." I've had some rich spiritual experience, but this was an awakening for me. I realized that my out-of-balance brain chemistry was leveling out.

This breakthrough brought me personal renewal and enabled me to function better, to address thought-pattern issues I needed to correct or renew. It gave me a chance for my emotions and thoughts to experience "normal" again. Looking back, I've wondered if I've *always* had some chemical imbalance that pushed me toward depression. Maybe it took the extreme pressure and stress of planting a new church to bring it fully to the surface.

It also helped my journey with depression when, in a prayer group, I met another pastor who also struggled with depression [that would be me, Gary]. It helped me realize that I wasn't different or weird. I was surprised at first when he told me he was taking meds too, but it helped me to realize that I wasn't damaged goods, and if I was, I wasn't alone! Being open about the problem has helped me keep tabs on my journey, and I've been able to help so many other people deal with their depression too.

A couple of times I decided I didn't need the meds anymore—that I was "cured," delivered, whatever. Each time, though, I was painfully reminded of what my doctor has told me: If it's a chemical imbalance, I may have to be on meds the rest of my life. [Rich and I will talk about this later in the book. Read on, pilgrim!]

Our first child's pediatrician was a committed Christ-follower. I remember when he first saw our little boy, who had a lot of health problems the first year of his life. After the introductions, he said, "I believe God is the healer. Sometimes He uses me and sometimes He bypasses me. It doesn't matter to me what He chooses to do, because He's the healer." Then he prayed for our son before examining him. I recall that story because that's the way I have to look at my journey with depression.

So today I took an antidepressant and loved God.

Mother Teresa wrote, "I am told God lives in me—and yet the reality of darkness and coldness and emptiness is so great that nothing touches my soul."[8] I found this statement on the Web, because my family doctor had said something to me about Mother Teresa's depression. When I went on-line to double-check the actual source of this statement, my Yahoo! search took me to this article, which is typical of the way Christians can sometimes "spiritualize" depression, making other believers depressed about being depressed.

> Mother Teresa, Daughter of God? [Note the question mark! The author of this article wonders if she is a true Christian. Here's his explanation:] My heart grew heavy as I read the recent story of one of the world's best known names—Mother Theresa . . . [L]etters by the famed charity worker were released which documented the condition of her spirit as she questioned her relationship with God. In the letters, written in the '50s & '60s, she made statements like, "In my soul, I can't tell you how dark it is, how painful, how terrible . . ." In the CNN story, Catholic leaders dismiss her feelings as those felt by all those who strive for a relationship with God. But according to the Word of God we are given an assurance of our salvation. We may feel like we're in a wilderness at times, but certainly, those who have accepted Jesus as Savior and Lord do not spend their lives feeling abandoned or disregarded by Him."[9]

We agree. Certainly, no one *should* spend his or her life feeling abandoned or disregarded by God. But what if they do? What if depression is a lifelong struggle? Is it a sign that they are not really a child of God? Does it mean that somehow the favor of God is not on them, or that they are being judged by God? Should we assume that they've allowed demonic influence to intrude into their lives, or that they don't have enough faith to claim the promises of God?

My dear uncle Martin had to leave full-time Christian ministry in his thirties. Forty years later, he's still receiving disability income from his denomination. To suggest my uncle is not a true believer because he hasn't been able to fully overcome his darkness is, in my view, cruel and unusual punishment. People who are depressed need to be encouraged, loved, and accepted . . . not scolded or condemned for something that can be as real for them as a physical disability is for a person in a wheelchair.

There's no condemnation for those who are in Christ Jesus—unless they're depressed or struggling with some other issue that Christians think shouldn't be a problem for Christians.

When people are misinformed about something, this is what happens. Unnecessary pain is inflicted because of misinformation, pain that compounds the pain of depression itself. That's why we must address the D-myths. Maybe we should have called them "Dumb Things Smart People Believe About Depression." Check them out in Appendix A. The list there, however, is not exhaustive. New myths, or new versions of old myths, arise all the time. They are as varied as the countless ways human beings can find to express ignorance, denial, confusion, and even pride.

A Light in the Dark

So is there hope? Yes!

Rich and I want to write about how we personally feel about depression. As you know by now, I can write about the subject as an "insider," and so can Rich. A pastor friend of mine, Mark Fuller, introduced me to Dr. Rich Jacobs. "Rich would be perfect to write a book with you on depression," he told me. "He's an MD, and he has a deep personal interest in the subject because his wife, Sue, has been emotionally paralyzed, even bedridden, with severe depression."

In this book, Rich and I will dispel the myths about depression and offer hope and healing from both biblical/pastoral and professional/clinical perspectives. This is not, however, a textbook. We are not "experts" in the field, although we've done our homework. We've made every effort to write about this subject correctly, intelligently, and sensitively.

We only know what we know based on our unique life experiences with depression, speaking with others, and reading extensively. We want this book to answer your questions, but mostly we are praying that our stories will touch your heart. Our earnest desire is that what we write will help you understand more deeply God's unconditional love for you, unmask the lies swirling around depression, and give you pathways to wholeness—steps you can take to live above depression. Depression is common—even "normal"—for many people. We want to take the bite out of this disease and help you understand it, face it, manage it, and overcome it.

In the chapters that follow, we will help you understand the basic components of human life—body, emotions, mind, and spirit—and how each of these elements can relate to the problem of depression.

There's hope. And you are not alone.

chapter 3

Depressed by What We Don't Know:

How to Recognize True Depression

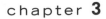

Morris would seek out Beau when the melancholy hit because Beau never asked why he suffered like that, why Morris couldn't just get up and walk away from whatever was bothering him.

—Edward P. Jones, *The Known World*

The only normal people are the ones you don't know very well.

—Alfred Adler, Austrian psychologist

Why are so many people depressed?

And if so many people are depressed, why do we understand so little about it?

As we explore some of the dark labyrinth of depression and seek to understand it better, Rich and I would like to warn you about the complexity of this subject. Like every good pharmaceutical company does when introducing their medicines, we want to make you aware of some possible side effects of using our book as a diagnostic tool.

No book can adequately address every aspect of a condition as complex as depression. And opinions about the subject are amazingly diverse. The many expressions of depression, and the possibilities for both cures and causes that we will mention may at times seem confusing. For instance, there are times (severe cases) when the attention of a medical professional is critical. In other people, there is every reason to believe that with prayer and good self-help tools, they can overcome their relatively minor symptoms of depression.

Sometimes the many avenues for treatment may even seem contradictory as we look at first one, then another possibility from one chapter to another. But in the mix of information available to you here, our hope is that *you can pick out the specific advice that best suits your situation* or the situation of someone you know and care about who suffers from this malady.

Like the little piece of paper that comes with your prescription, this "disclaimer" doesn't mean that you should not take the medicine. Just take it advisedly. The presentations of depression are *highly* complex and multilayered. This reality makes diagnosis and treatment challenging, and sometimes hit-and-miss.

But don't let its complexity discourage you. There are real helps available to those who suffer from depression. We hope our stories, and the stories of many others, will encourage you to press on until you find what works for you.

In the first chapter we looked at Rich and Sue's encounter with depression, and in the second chapter, I told you my story (I'll continue with my story later on in this chapter).

This chapter and the one following are designed to throw a little light on the most common presentations of depression, helping you to distinguish between what is just a "down" mood or season of life and what may constitute actual depression. We toss this word around a lot in our society. It's no wonder we are often unclear about what it really means. Experiencing sadness, grief, and anxiety does not mean a person is depressed. They may at times go together, but not necessarily.

The main difference is *duration*. Normal anxiety or sadness are temporary. They generally pass within a reasonable time—depending on the nature and extent of the threat or loss—without any clinical intervention. Although these emotions are intrusive, they are not destructive. In some instances, the guidance that these emotions (anxiety, grief, sadness) provide can actually benefit us. Depression, however, is an entirely different story. Maybe the following testimonies will make the distinction a little clearer.

Sad, but Not Depressed

Cole anxiously awaited the final verdict. It had been an arduous and nerve-wracking process. First, there was the notice that the Internal Revenue Service was going to audit him. Then Cole had to find, assemble, and organize his financial records to defend his case. Finally, there was the audit interview with the IRS examiner. Cole could tell things were not going well for him. The auditor kept asking questions Cole couldn't answer. The frown on the auditor's face spoke volumes. Cole owed the IRS another $8,633!

To pay his obligation, Cole emptied his savings account and took out a small loan. His dream of buying a new home vanished, as the down payment he had been saving up for years went to Uncle Sam. He spent the rest of the month feeling dejected and blue. In time, however, Cole was able to sit down with an accountant to plan how to rebuild his finances and buy his dream house. Cole was glum about his setback, but he was also planning his future.

Jeanette's phone rang. It was 3:14 in the morning. Something had to be wrong. When Jeanette answered the telephone, she heard weeping at the other end of the line. She recognized her mother's voice immediately.

"Jeanie," her mom said, "we just received a call from the county hospital. Your sister, Milly, was killed in an auto accident tonight. Can you please come over to the house now, honey? Your dad and I need you."

Jeanette's feelings of grief and mourning continued for a little more than a month after Milly's funeral, but she had to return to work after only one week. The distraction of her duties and the companionship of her friends at work seemed to help Jeanette. But in her private moments, she couldn't help but remember her sister— their times as children growing up together, their petty spats, shared adventures, and joyful fellowship. These were tearful times for her. In the midst of her tears she would sometimes smile. She'd had a wonderful sister. Jeanette would miss her greatly.

Marriage counseling didn't help. Their pastor couldn't work a miracle either. After two years of arguments and disagreements, Sophie's husband, Dustin, decided to run off with another woman. Now the divorce proceedings were complete. Sophie would receive alimony and child support from Dustin. She retained custody of their two children and the house, but she felt tired, empty, and "depressed." It seemed that the "other woman" had been part of their marital problem all along.

In spite of herself, Sophie kept asking herself if there wasn't something else she could or should have done to save her marriage. She knew this kind of thinking was irrational. She had been a good wife and mother. Dustin was the cause of their divorce—he was the one who had broken their wedding vows.

Sophie made new friends in the church's singles group. Although being a single parent was more difficult, Sophie began to make a new life for herself and her children. As she established new routines, Sophie found the peace and happiness that eluded her during her divorce.

Cole, Jeanette, and Sophie all experienced events in their lives that caused them anxiety, sorrow, mourning, or sadness. None of them had clinical depression. The normal distress of our emotional life is a spectrum that runs from anxiety at one extreme, to sadness at the other. Every person has a body, a soul, and a spirit—and each of these components has needs that must be met in order for the person to experience wholeness.

When we perceive a threat to the supply of our needs, whether the threat is real or imaginary, we experience normal anxiety. Recall that Cole was anxious as he contemplated the threat to his finances from the IRS. In addition, we experience sadness when the supply of our need is lost. Cole became dejected and blue when he lost his financial security because of the payment he had to make to the IRS. Jeanette and Sophie both experienced significant losses in their lives that caused sorrow or mourning.

Anxiety and sorrow, when they are within their normal ranges, give us guidance and assistance. *They are sentinels that warn us to change our behavior or thinking to accommodate changes in our environment.* They motivate us to reassess our lives. Anxiety is the adrenalin-driven emotion that prepares us to fight back or run when we feel endangered. Cole's anxiety motivated him to put his financial papers together and build a defense for his IRS audit.

Experiencing sadness or mourning, on the other hand, is normally a time of reflection in which we assess our new situation following a loss. Also, *it is a time to think about and learn from the past.* Consider Sophie, who evaluated her performance as a wife and mother during her melancholy. This allowed her to free herself from unreasonable self-recrimination. Jeanette remembered her sister and their times together. Her bereavement was a psychological and spiritual process by which she released the bonds and attachment with the sister she loved and lost, enabling her to eventually move on with life.

More Than Sadness: Bill's Story

Marci took her last breath at 5:35 AM on Wednesday, November 23. She was "only" sixty-three years old, young by today's standards. Her family was gathered around Marci's bed to spend their last moments with her. Each family member took turns reading aloud Marci's favorite Bible verses. During moments of silence, someone would begin singing one of her treasured hymns. As Marci's breathing became irregular and the rigors of death gripped her frail body, even this faith-filled family became distressed. The end came peacefully, but grief over the loss of a beloved mother and wife was crushing. They all loved her greatly.

In the months that preceded Marci's death, the family earnestly sought a cure for her at prayer meetings and in healing services. But Marci just got weaker. Her doctors promised a breakthrough from a new chemotherapy treatment, yet Marci's lymphoma kept growing. The radiation treatments didn't help either. The family heard stories of others who were recovering from their illnesses. They even witnessed a miraculous healing of one of their friends at church. But Marci dwindled away. Her blood tests became progressively more abnormal. She was losing her battle against cancer, yet she had a radiant calm throughout her ordeal. She knew it was her time.

At last, her family admitted that only divine intervention would save Marci's life. They enrolled her in a hospice program that provided much-needed support and assistance. Eight weeks later Marci went to be with the Lord. She was finally at rest, but her husband, Bill, was exhausted.

Bill was Marci's principal caregiver during the last months of her life. He drove her to the doctors, sat with her day and night in the hospital, and fed her when she was too weak to eat. Bill did the laundry, kept the house, paid the bills, and tried to live a normal life. And he prayed, night and day, whenever he could, that his wife would be cured. But Marci did not even live to celebrate their forty-fifth wedding anniversary. Her relatively young age seemed to make the tragedy of her loss greater.

Bill endured Marci's funeral and the condolences of family and friends in a numbed state of shock. When he returned to an empty house filled with memories of his beloved wife, he tumbled into deep depression. The accumulated stresses of taking care of a sick wife for eighteen months, attending to all the household duties, and the loss of his Marci, took their toll on Bill. But it was the funeral and returning to his empty house that was the final straw. Bill was mentally, emotionally, physically, and spiritually spent.

At first, Bill's kids thought he was in simple mourning, a normal grief that is expected after the loss of a loved one. However, they eventually came to suspect that something else was wrong with Dad. They just didn't know what it was. Bill didn't know what was wrong either. What's more, he really didn't care. He was frequently tearful, spoke often of joining his wife in heaven, and lost over twenty pounds. His house also fell into disrepair. The family finally became alarmed when his daughter visited him one afternoon to find an empty refrigerator and Bill in bed sleeping.

Eventually, Bill's thoughts and speech became jumbled. He had difficulty concentrating, and his memory was impaired. He couldn't balance his checkbook even if he felt like it, because simple arithmetic was impossible for him. So his bills went unpaid. And he began to see and hear things that weren't really there. More than two years following his wife's death, Bill was not just blue; he was badly confused. Bill had a condition called psychotic depression.

Bill was hospitalized and given intensive medical attention. He soon recovered some normal function, but in spite of several different antidepressant medications and counseling, Bill remained depressed for another eight months. The loving support and prayers of family and friends were eventually welcomed by him. (Before, he regarded them as unwelcome intrusions.) After a full year of being depression-free, Bill's medication was gradually reduced and discontinued without difficulty. Although Bill still experienced episodes of grief and sorrow over the loss of his wife, he could cope with life again. He was a whole, productive person. Bill's family had their father back again. Bill had his life back.

His story is not that uncommon. A loss or tragedy can sometimes trigger depression. Often, the accumulative impact of many stresses brings a person over the edge of simple sorrow into the chasm of depression. But for others, no "final straw" is evident. The depression just gathers in them for no apparent reason.

Just "in Me"

For most of my life, I (Gary) have suffered off and on with low-level chronic depression. I'm in my midfifties now, but I can remember back to times in high school and college when, for no good reason, I felt melancholy. I've always been ambitious, but my mother remembers when I would just lie there on our old brown sofa. Troubled. "What's wrong?" she would ask. "I really don't know," I'd tell her.

I'm grateful that my depression has never been debilitating; I've never missed a day of work because of it. However, getting up in the morning and going to the office has been extraordinarily difficult at times. For many years, I woke up daily with morning darkness. Only pressing forward into the day seemed to let the sun shine into my soul. Activity has been therapy for me, but the downside is that, for most of my life, I've been overactive: leading a huge church, traveling often to speak at conferences, and writing books in my spare time! Someone on my church staff asked me recently, "Do you ever sleep at night?"

Overwork and stress make my depression worse, as have the darker seasons of my life, but my depression is not primarily related to circumstances. It's just "in me." It's been in my mother's side of the family for generations. I mentioned in the second chapter that my uncle had to leave full-time pastoral ministry because of disabling depression. I have pleasant memories of staying at his home in Minneapolis when I was about fifteen. He was very good to me. Along with his depression, he had insomnia, and being a night owl myself, I remember sitting with him at his '50s-style chrome-and-Formica kitchen table—and watching him smoke a cigarette for some feeling of relief. Some Lutheran pastors do that, and it wasn't as much of a stigma in the early '60s. Perhaps it's experiences like this that have made me more accepting of myself and others who suffer with depression.

People who don't have a problem with depression, though, have difficulty understanding those who do. *Everyone* gets down from time to time, usually because something difficult, even terrible, has happened. Lose your job or someone you love, or face a serious health crisis, and you will be depressed. This is what professionals call "acute depression"—a sudden and perhaps prolonged personal soul distress caused by a specific painful event. For example, my mother was treated with antidepressants when my father died. For a while you feel like you are dying inside, but as time passes you recover and return to a fairly normal life.

Depression and sadness overlap,[1] but they are not exactly the same. There are many instances, of course, of people who remain depressed for many years as a result of an actuating event, but generally when someone has had a major loss they eventually recover.

"Chronic depression," however, like chronic pain, lingers. It may be a low-level, sub-surface pain, but it's always there. Doctors call this dysthymia, and as I mentioned above, pressure and stress can make it worse, much like physical exertion can make a back problem worse.

Fortunately, both acute and chronic depression can be treated with medication, because depression is not "just an emotional problem." As Dr. Rich will explain in more detail in chapter 5, depression is often a serious chemical imbalance in the brain. If this is the case, certain drugs can give dramatic help. Rich will probably squirm when he reads this, but to me, medication for depression is like WD-40 for a squeaky brain. It takes the rust out of the receptors. You can't just shake it off. It's not just a negative emotion or a demon.

Epilepsy is another brain malfunction that people once thought was demon possession. Rich and I believe in the possibility of demon influence in people's lives, and we will talk about this in some depth later on in the book. But folks with epilepsy need medication and compassion from those who interact with them, not judgment and censure. Family members and friends who fully understand what's happening when they're having a seizure are crucial. The same is true with depression. The right medication and other treatment, as well as informed and compassionate caregivers, are key to recovery.

Shame on Me

When someone first suggested that antidepressant medication would help me, I balked. Most of my life, I simply resigned myself to my problem. My depression was unpleasant, but it wasn't debilitating, so I just put up with it. When I finally decided to ask my doctor for meds, I felt uncomfortable talking to him about the problem. But he not only gave me a prescription, he also gave me permission to take the medication, confessing that he took it too! A God-minded man, he told me he had thought a lot about depression and had concluded that it's not just about people like us cursed with some mental aberration. He believes more and more people are depressed because our "civilized" world has become increasingly complex and stressful, which depletes our serotonin levels.

We long for a simpler life, a simpler time. Certainly country folk in the past had depression too, but we have upped the ante with the craziness of our urban world. Just driving to work is maddening! My doctor added, "The way we live just isn't the way God created us to live." I couldn't agree more.

Think about Adam and Eve. Now think about your office space, your apartment, and your car. Presently, I'm at a lovely retreat center where I do most of my writing. I'm 125 miles from home . . . *with car trouble*. It's in the garage here in the small town of Cottonwood, getting a new alternator. It's been there *three days*, because the first alternator they ordered was the wrong part, and minutes ago they called to inform me that a *second* replacement alternator didn't work. Since I'm nearly finished with my writing, I'll have to take a bus back to Phoenix. At this moment I have no idea how I'm going to get my car back. Hassles, man, hassles . . . it's depressing!

A few years ago, I heard an interview on National Public Radio about a "cure" for depression: work for a year on a Norwegian farm in northern Minnesota. I couldn't get to Minnesota, so I started taking medication. It has really helped. After a couple of years, though, I started neglecting it. My life felt good and I felt good. It even felt like I was feeling better *without* the medication, but that was a myth. I went back to my doctor and told him I was struggling again. I have to confess: *I hated to do that.* Even though I've been taking medication most of the last six years, I *always* feel awkward and a little ashamed to hand my prescription to the pharmacist. Or if I have to list medications I'm taking on a medical history report for a new doctor or specialist, it's easier for me to talk about the colonoscopy I had last year than it is to discuss my depression meds! Yet the benefits of the medication far outweigh my moments of fleeting shame, and one of those benefits is talking and writing about these issues to help others—like you!

Meds, though, aren't Nirvana. Drugs have helped me, but I've had to do other things to keep healthy, like exercise regularly and set boundaries for my life, especially my work. Depression is a complex problem that involves not only brain chemistry, but my past, family systems, lifestyle, other medications I may be taking, the way I think about God and faith, and my diet, exercise, and sleep patterns. People with depression can be hurt and helped by all kinds of things, which is why we want to present a comprehensive approach to understanding and treating depression.

With a better understanding of the difference between periodic sadness, anxiety, and mourning—all of which can be normal in the right circumstances—and chronic depression, which is a serious and treatable disease, we are ready to identify the symptoms of true depression.

Indicators of True Depression

The technical definition for major depression (what we usually just call "depression") is defined by the American Psychiatric Association as follows:[2]

At least five of the following findings are present during the same two-week period and represent a *change* from the person's previous function. At least one of the symptoms must be either depressed mood or loss of interest or pleasure.

- Depressed mood most of the day, nearly every day. Children and adolescents can present with an irritable mood.
- Markedly diminished interest or pleasure in all, or almost all, activities most of the day, nearly every day.
- Significant weight loss (when not dieting) or weight gain; or a decrease or increase in appetite nearly every day.
- Insomnia or hypersomnia (excessive sleepiness) nearly every day.
- Psychomotor agitation or retardation (being agitated or moving slowly) nearly every day.
- Fatigue or loss of energy nearly every day.
- Feelings of worthlessness or excessive or inappropriate guilt nearly every day.
- Diminished ability to think or concentrate, or indecisiveness, nearly every day.
- Recurrent thoughts of death (not just fear of dying), recurrent suicidal ideation without a specific plan, or a suicide attempt or a specific plan for committing suicide.

In addition, before physicians diagnose major depression, they must exclude depressive symptoms due to drugs, alcohol, or medication. It is also important to rule out symptoms caused by bereavement of less than two months' duration.

Although anxiety and sorrow may not be pleasant emotions, they serve a useful purpose. They are constructive emotions that serve the needs of our souls. When the loss is great, such as the death of a loved one, the sorrow can be so distracting and disruptive that it can disturb someone's appetite, sleep, and daily routine. Although this can cause some weight loss, insomnia, or disorganization, the *intensity of normal grief and sorrow does not ordinarily endanger the health and well-being of the person.* Normal anxiety, grief, and sorrow are not pathological. They are not maladaptive. They are not diseases.

A Destructive and Progressive Affliction

Depression, on the other hand, can develop from personal loss or stress, but it can also arise without any apparent provocation. Depression is *not* a constructive adaptation to a threat or loss. It is destructive and often progressive. It is not simply an emotion; it impairs the physical health of the person who suffers from it. Its intensity and duration are more severe than is found with sadness, grief, or mourning. Although anxiety and sadness are at either end of the normal emotional spectrum, it is not normal for us to spend most of our time there. Depression abides; relentlessly, it cuts deeply into the soul.

Depression affects people emotionally and spiritually. People with depression often believe that God has abandoned them. They are vulnerable to spiritual attack and bondage from disparaging thought patterns. People with depression often have a hopelessness that makes death seem preferable to life. Suicide, and sometimes homicide, is a risk with depression. When depression becomes severe, people find it difficult to think or concentrate. They may even experience delusions and hallucinations. Responsible choices and decisions become difficult. Social relationships break down. This undermining of the health and wholeness of a person is the principal differentiating factor that separates clinical depression from emotions like sorrow or sadness.

Depression also affects our more complex "soulish" functions. People with depression suffer from groundless feelings of guilt and inadequacy. Self-recrimination and a sense of worthlessness can give

way to hopelessness. Withdrawal from other people and social isolation is common, so depression disrupts marriages, friendships, and
other family relationships. Depression is a lonely illness. This is part
of the desolation it causes.

A family history of depression is helpful in recognizing its presence. So is a personal or family history of alcohol or substance abuse.
Many people with depression do not know they are sick, but they
feel terrible. For this reason, some people with depression resort to
drugs or alcohol to relieve their symptoms. Unfortunately, alcohol
and most drugs ultimately make depression worse.

Many different diseases have symptoms that masquerade as
depression. Depression has atypical forms that require their own
technical diagnostic criteria. Children and adolescents can look more
agitated and angry than sad when they suffer from depression.
Some forms of depression even have episodes of giddiness, euphoria,
or mania that alternate with the melancholy. We'll talk more about
this in the next chapter.

The important point is that depression is not grief. It is not sadness. It is not a person feeling sorry for themselves. Rather, the serious disease known as depression strikes at the welfare of body, spirit,
and soul. In other words, it affects every part of us as human beings.
That's what makes treating it so tricky.

No Easy Answers

With some understanding of the physical and spiritual causes of
depression, it makes no sense to insist that depression is merely a
character flaw. When we understand the desolation that depression
causes the human soul, it is absurd to demand that people with
depression simply need to "snap out of" their illness. When we
are clear about the differences between sadness and depression,
it is cruel and uncaring to expect those with depression to "pull

themselves up by their own bootstraps." The more we learn about depression, the more we become equipped to deal with it constructively.

We also must be careful not to focus all of our thinking on one aspect of the manifestations. For example, as Christians we can be guilty of "over-spiritualizing" our approach to depression, thinking that faith alone is the key to overcoming it. While depression certainly has significant spiritual elements (discussed further in chapter 6), we have to remember that God made us with physical bodies that have material needs. When we're hungry we eventually need to eat. When we are thirsty we need to drink. No reasonable person would suggest that if I'm thirsty or hungry I just need to pray more! In the same way, depression has implications for our physical needs that we must meet by material means. Although it is essential to seek healing through prayer and petition, it is unreasonable to refuse medication just because it isn't a spiritual intervention.

In a similar way, it is unwise to rely only on medication for healing from depression. Our spiritual selves should be involved in the treatment. Although the empirical studies are contradictory, depending on the agenda of the investigators, research shows that prayer and counseling improves the therapeutic outcomes,[3] and patients with depression respond better with medication *and* counseling, rather than just medication alone.[4]

Sickness and injury are humbling because we must admit that we are ill. We often need to seek the help of others to get better. It is important for us not to let pride keep us from doing this when we are depressed. It is also important not to become arrogant toward others who may be experiencing depression. When we impose a stigma on this disease and its treatment, we compound the hurt they already experience. Depression sufferers need humble compassion and loving assistance from us, not condemnation.

Finally, few people know everything about depression. Each of us has our own part to play. The psychiatrist is expert in using medication. The clinical psychologist provides behavioral and cognitive therapy. Pastors are best equipped to help with spiritual needs. Moreover, no one understands the effects of depression more than the people who suffer from it. For this reason, group therapy with others who suffer from depression is often helpful. All of us can help by providing love and support to those who have this illness.

Human beings are complex creatures. The causes and consequences of depression are varied. This requires a multidisciplinary, team-approach to dealing with depression that actually improves clinical outcomes.[5] If it is humbling to ask one person for help, it may be humiliating to ask many people for assistance. However, *this is the very thing that we must do when we are depressed.*

When we set aside our misconceptions about depression and learn more about its causes and effects, we become equipped to help those who suffer from it. When we reject the stigmas associated with depression and its treatment, we create the freedom people need to get the help they require.

In the next chapter we will give a brief overview of the most common expressions of depression.

chapter 4

The Many Faces of Depression:

Overview of the Most Common Types

As more people recognize that these illnesses are treatable, more are rediscovering their sense of optimism and purpose through appropriate treatment.

—U.S. News: BEST HEALTH ON-LINE

A disease that only causes sadness in the winter. An affliction that strikes after the joyous time of childbirth. A condition that causes our emotions to swing erratically up and down. A malady that ceaselessly oppresses the soul. An ailment that brings destructive, irritable melancholy. What do all these have in common? Depression!

One of the unusual things about depression is that it is both a disease and the dominant symptom of many unrelated diseases. When we talk about depression, we are usually talking about "major depression." Major depression is named after the melancholy that characterizes this ailment, but there is a whole menagerie of unrelated physical, psychological, and spiritual conditions that make people depressed. In fact, major depression may be several conditions rather than just a single abnormality. To complicate matters even more, the best treatment for each of these different diseases can vary, even though the symptoms are the same. It's not unusual for doctors to make the wrong treatment call with a patient the first or second time.

It's impossible for this book to explore every disease associated with depression. It doesn't even explore everything about major depression. Instead, we offer information that dispels the commonly held misconceptions about depression that are harmful and deceptive. Hopefully, the following discussion will at least give an overview that can help shed a little light on a multifaceted problem.

1. Endless gloom: dysthymia

Natalie couldn't ever remember a time when she didn't feel depressed. Her struggles with too little energy, disturbed sleep, and feelings of low self-esteem began in high school. Every day, during the fourteen years since then, Natalie has felt sadness for no reason.

While in high school, Natalie didn't have hobbies or interests like the other kids. She didn't enjoy parties or hanging around with her friends. She just felt tired and blue all the time. She also felt like a failure. God felt far away.

Natalie's parents took her to see the family doctor when she was eighteen years old. The physical exam and all the test results were normal. Natalie didn't feel normal, though. Worse yet, Natalie's parents thought she was lazy and malingering. Her friends thought she was a hypochondriac.

The day after her thirty-second birthday, Natalie saw a television program about dysthymia. She immediately recognized her condition. Her family physician referred Natalie to a psychiatrist who confirmed the diagnosis. Natalie was started on an antidepressant medication, but that only helped a little. Finally, she began psychotherapy. The supportive counseling eased her feelings of hopelessness and guilt. The cognitive therapy addressed the negative thinking patterns she had developed over the years. With this treatment, Natalie learned to set realistic goals for herself, think less pessimistically, and be less critical of herself and others.

Natalie also received behavioral therapy that gave her better interpersonal and coping skills. She learned to solve conflicts constructively with family members and friends. Problem-solving counseling helped her solve financial and work problems that were adding stress to her life. Finally, weekly meetings with her singles group pastor helped Natalie cling to God's Word and live in His truth. All of this made a difference. After about six months of counseling and medication, Natalie began to have some good days along with the bad days—a real sign of progress. She was on the road to recovery, but she knew it would be a long battle for her. Still, for the first time, Natalie had hope.

Natalie's story is typical for people suffering from dysthymia. Dysthymia is a chronic, low-level depression that can persist for years without relief. The diagnosis is made when someone suffers from depression almost daily for at least two years. All of the typical findings of major depression are not usually present and the depression itself is often much milder. It's important to keep in mind, though, that it is possible for major depression to develop in people with dysthymia.

Apathy, fatigue, and an inability to enjoy the activities of life are typical for dysthymia. So are problems with concentrating, negative thoughts, poor self-esteem, self-criticism, guilt, and irritability. The depression of dysthymia disturbs the simple things in life, like sleeping, eating, walking, and even talking. Social withdrawal and an absent libido are common.[1]

Natalie did the right thing in seeing her family doctor first.

Someone with Natalie's symptoms should first be evaluated for glandular conditions, like hypothyroidism or adrenal insufficiency. Anemia, kidney failure, and other serious medical problems should also be excluded. When this has been done, psychiatric or psychological evaluation should begin. Although antidepressant medication[2] can help dysthymia, psychotherapy is just as important.[3] This is because dysthymia causes serious disruption in both behavioral and thought patterns. These patterns must be corrected before full recovery occurs. There is no cure for dysthymia at this time, but medication and counseling can restore meaning, hope, and joy to life again, as it did for Natalie.

2. Up and down: bipolar disease

The phone rang just as the evening news was about to begin. It was Kaitlyn, one of the people who regularly attended the Sunday school class I taught.

"Rich, I need to meet with you to talk about some problems I'm having. Can you please meet me for dinner this week? This is urgent!"

Kaitlyn sounded distressed. She had never called me at home before, and her call perplexed me.

"Can you please tell me what this is about, Kaitlyn?" I asked.

"I'd rather not talk about it over the phone," she replied. "Please, I need to talk to you. This is very important! It's about my husband, Randy, and about things going on at church."

Kaitlyn and her husband had been members of our church for many years. They were active in several ministries and strong in their faith. I tried to find out more information over the phone, but she remained adamant that she must talk to me in person. She also refused to talk to anyone on our church's pastoral staff. I finally agreed to have dinner with her on the condition that my wife, Sue, also be allowed to attend.

Sue and I met Kaitlyn at the local Chinese restaurant the next evening. She was already there when we arrived, a full ten minutes early, looking jittery, agitated, and disheveled. She also looked somewhat frightened.

We ordered our meal, then I asked, "What can I help you with, Kaitlyn?"

She began a long and complicated story of imagined and unsubstantiated intrigues, betrayals, and suspicions. She had pressured speech—one word quickly followed the next without the normal pauses or inflection. Her sentences were incomplete and jumbled, resembling free-association. As I listened to her rambling discourse, I prayed that God would help me understand why I was meeting with her and how I could help. It was in the midst of my prayers that God gave me the needed insight.

I stopped Kaitlyn after about fifteen minutes. "Kaitlyn, do you have bipolar disease?" I asked.

Her eyes widened, and her mouth dropped open slightly. "Why yes, I do," she said. "How did you know?"

I explained, "I think your bipolar illness is acting up now. I think you need to have your medication adjusted. This may be the explanation for all your concerns."

Kaitlyn went on to tell me that she stopped taking her Lithium, a medication used to treat bipolar disease. She said she felt good and didn't think she needed it anymore. Fortunately, she accepted my advice and saw her doctor that week. After about four weeks of taking her medication again, Kaitlyn was back to normal. Many of the relationship problems that she was having vanished.

Kaitlyn's condition, bipolar disease, was formerly known as manic-depressive psychosis. Bipolar disease afflicts about two million people in the United States. It is a serious illness that tends to run in families, although no specific genetic defect has been discovered yet.[4] It affects men and women with about equal frequency. Often the disease first presents as simple depression and is misdiagnosed as major depression. It may not fully reveal itself for years. Bipolar disease typically begins in adolescence or early adulthood.[5] When it occurs in children, it is often misdiagnosed as attention-deficit/hyperactivity disorder.[6] Its cause is unknown.

Kaitlyn was not depressed the evening Sue and I met with her to have dinner. Instead, she was having a manic episode. Bipolar disease can look just like depression for a while, but eventually at least one manic episode arises to make the diagnosis of bipolar disease. Sometimes the medical treatment of the depression can unmask the mania to reveal the real illness.

Although depression is a debilitating condition, the mania part of this disease is often far more destructive. People may display inappropriate risk-taking behavior, develop drug and alcohol abuse, and exhibit sexual promiscuity. These behaviors can lead to financial loss from unrestricted spending or gambling, drug dependencies, criminal or legal problems, broken relationships and marriages, and even suicide. People feel great during the early stages of their mania. They report feeling invincible, expansive, optimistic, and giddy. They need little sleep, feel capable of doing anything, and accomplish prodigious amounts of work. In time, however, the mania usually makes orderly thoughts difficult. The manic person becomes agitated and has difficulty concentrating. His or her judgment becomes seriously impaired. Amazingly, all of this can happen in bipolar individuals without their even knowing they have a problem!

Supportive counseling can help repair disrupted marriages and relationships that occur during the manic episodes. Financial and legal counseling may also be required. The most important component of the treatment of bipolar disease is medication, however.[7] Doctors recommend preventative medication for people with bipolar disease because it is a chronic, lifelong condition.[8] It is important for family members and friends to be vigilant since the disease may flare up without its victim being aware of it. Telltale signs include rapid speech, disorganized thoughts, insomnia, elevated mood, excessive industriousness, risk-taking behavior, and poor judgment.

Medical non-compliance—not following their doctor's instructions—is a problem with bipolar disease. People feel great during the early part of the manic phase. This is the time when they often stop taking their medicine. The condition can require periodic adjustments in treatment even when people faithfully take their medicines. Although no cure for bipolar disease is known, a good quality of life can occur with treatment and support.

3. Sullen anger and distant moodiness: depression in adolescents

D in English, D in American History, F in Algebra, and Cs in everything else. This was Connor's worst report card ever. It was a shock to his parents because Connor had been an honor student at Central High School last year.

"Connor, what is it with this report card?" his mother asked. Connor's dad was just silent. He was tired of fighting with Connor about homework and school. Connor was silent too. He didn't know what was wrong.

The family was very worried about their oldest child. Over the last five months, he seemed more irritable, angry, sullen, withdrawn, and unruly. Uncharacteristically, he began to have temper tantrums when asked to do his chores or accompany the family on outings. Football had always been Connor's great love in school, but he didn't go out for the football team this year, even though he lettered in the sport last year. And he dropped out of the school's concert band, even though he won the first chair, first clarinet spot last year.

Connor began to complain about going to church each Sunday. Moreover, he tried to stay home from school during the week because he "didn't feel well." When a complete physical examination by their family doctor failed to find any abnormality, Connor's parents began to contemplate restricting his privileges and punishing him for his school grades and behavior. Then they found his suicide note.

Connor was at school when his mom found a spiral notebook under his bed while she was vacuuming. The notebook was filled with macabre death poems and an episodic diary of Connor's thoughts and feelings. In this notebook, Connor talked about his crying episodes, his hopelessness, and his secret death wishes. Obviously, Connor was a very unhappy young man.

About 4 to 5 percent of teens experience depression. Connor's depression is a typical presentation for adolescents. Plummeting school grades, social withdrawal, and irritable, unruly behavior are common in adolescent depression. The *change in behavior* is the key clue that depression may be present. Another clue is a family history of depression. Although use of illicit drugs can cause a similar picture, drug and alcohol use is also part of the typical presentation of adolescents with depression. When drug abuse occurs, it is important to look deeper to see if underlying depression is lurking undetected.

The issue of teen suicide is worth emphasizing. About seven hundred thousand high school students will attempt suicide each year. Girls have a greater suicide risk than boys; the reason for this is unknown. Adolescents with a history of previous suicide attempts are at high risk for future attempts. Impulsive risk-taking behavior and suicide are both prominent features of teen depression. For this reason, one should not take adolescents' talking of suicide lightly. Behaviors suspicious for suicide include talking about death or wanting to die, suicidal thoughts, fantasies or plans, and giving away personal possessions.

An adolescent with a friend who attempted suicide is also at risk. If you suspect depression in a teenager, it is valuable to ask them directly if they are considering suicide. Never agree to keep a discussion about suicide with a teen confidential. If an adolescent is suicidal, it is vital to seek professional help immediately and take appropriate precautions. It is often advisable to hospitalize suicidal teens.

The medical treatment of adolescents with depression does not differ markedly from that of adults. Antidepressant medication is very helpful but, like adults, the risk for suicide may actually rise in teens at the beginning of treatment. It is important to watch teens more closely during this stage of therapy.

Counseling is very helpful to teenagers as well. Adolescence is a challenging and difficult time of life as it is. Many kids with depression are insecure and have a desperate desire to be liked and accepted by their peer group. A poor test score, a perceived slight from a friend or schoolmate, being bullied at school, or even an unanticipated disappointment can start a process that pushes a vulnerable teen into depression. Psychotherapy and counseling help adolescents cope with these issues. With proper treatment, the prognosis for most teens is excellent.

4. Winter blues: seasonal affective disorder (SAD)

One hundred and forty-seven pounds!

This was an all-time high weight record for Whitney. She had been gaining weight since mid-September. Now, as the end of

January approached, Whitney's distress over her recent weight gain didn't deter her from munching on her second Snickers candy bar that day. Since moving to Detroit from Miami, Florida, five years ago, Whitney noticed that she would get the "blahs" in the fall and the "blues" by midwinter. Cold overcast mornings made getting out of bed practically impossible. This year, Whitney's melancholy and misery seemed as bad as the unusually gloomy Detroit winter. She worried she would not make it to spring, when she knew from experience her sadness would go away.

Whitney is one of ten million Americans who suffers from Seasonal Affective Disorder (SAD). Her symptoms are typical: winter depression, weight gain, craving sweets or starchy foods, and other symptoms of depression that all disappear with the sunny days of spring or summer.

Women suffer from SAD more than men do.[9] It also tends to run in families.[10] Scientists have discovered that SAD has something to do with the daily duration and brightness of ambient light. People who live farther north have shorter fall and winter days; they also have more SAD.

The cause of SAD is unknown, but one theory links it to a change in melatonin secretion from the pineal gland, which resides at the base of the brain. Melatonin is a hormone that influences our daily wake-sleep cycle (circadian rhythm). Excessive secretion of melatonin may cause clinical depression in vulnerable people. Longer, brighter spring or summer days may decrease melatonin secretion and relieve the SAD symptoms, but the melatonin theory is far from certain.[11] Some research suggests that decreases in brain serotonin levels cause SAD.[12] For this reason, some physicians insist that SAD is not very different from major depression.

The association between reduced light and SAD suggests light as treatment. Bright light (about 10,000 lux) for thirty minutes per day can help some patients with SAD. Some people find a dimmer light (about 2500 lux) more acceptable, but longer light exposure is required.[13] Light treatment increases brain serotonin levels.[14] This may explain its effectiveness.

You can buy a commercially made light box for anywhere from $300 to $750. It is wise to consult your physician and obtain a medical and psychiatric evaluation before using a light box. If the weather permits, a daily brisk walk at midday combines the beneficial effects of light exposure with exercise. Light exposure is important, but it need not include the full spectrum of the sun. In fact, it is best to avoid the ultraviolet portion of light to prevent sunburn and skin cancer. Recent research suggests that light given very early in the morning ("dawn treatment") may be more effective than bright light given later in the day.[15]

Not everyone with SAD responds well to light treatment. When light treatment fails, antidepressant medication becomes the mainstay of treatment. As usual, exercise and proper nutrition are also important. When all other forms of treatment fail, most patients with SAD gain significant relief, or even complete resolution of their condition, by moving to sunnier climes where days are longer and brighter.

5. Untimely sadness: postpartum depression

"When you talk about postpartum, you can have people today, women, and what you do is you use vitamins. There is a hormonal thing that is going on, scientifically, you can prove that. But when you talk about emotional, chemical imbalances in people, there is no science behind that. You can use vitamins to help a woman through those things."[16]

With this statement, Tom Cruise startled the world by announcing that he knew the cause and cure of postpartum depression—the depression some moms experience after childbirth: *All we need is more vitamins!*

His remarks were directed at another celebrity, Brooke Shields, who experienced postpartum depression that required medical treatment. Her condition was so serious that she actually thought about killing her child. I heard her interviewed some months ago on National Public Radio. As they asked her questions about her trauma and her new book, she spoke honestly about her pain—and how she could not have survived without medications. Ms. Shields wrote, "I'm going to take a wild guess and say that Mr. Cruise has never suffered from postpartum depression. His comments are a disservice to mothers everywhere."[17] And to others, we might add, who suffer with a chemical imbalance. In a sidebar in a follow-up interview with Cruise, *Entertainment Weekly* reported that 61 percent of the American public liked Tom Cruise *less* as a result of his insensitive comments.[18]

Granted, nutrition and exercise are necessary for a healthy lifestyle. And they can ease the symptoms of depression. We will discuss this more in a later chapter. Postpartum depression, however, is a serious medical condition that we should not ignore. Symptoms include sadness, fatigue, insomnia, appetite changes, reduced libido, crying episodes, anxiety, and irritability. The condition is surprisingly common. Current data suggests that 5 to 9 percent of women will develop postpartum depression.[19] Because of the misconceptions and biases associated with depression (D-myths), less than one in five of these women will seek professional help.[20]

Postpartum depression, when it occurs, begins sometime during the first several months after childbirth. Some evidence suggests the depression can begin earlier than this, during the last trimester of pregnancy.[21] Although about half of all pregnant women develop irritability, melancholy, and insomnia during the first few days following birth, most of these symptoms typically disappear within two weeks.[22] Other women, unfortunately, go on to experience full-blown postpartum depression. This is especially true of women who become depressed while pregnant.

There is no evidence that vitamin deficiency has anything to do with postpartum depression. Scientists suspect that the cause of this condition may be related in some way to hormonal changes. Weak scientific data correlates dramatic hormonal shifts in women with depression.[23] Scientists were able to induce depression in some women during experiments by manipulating their hormones.[24] However, *scientific proof that hormonal changes cause the depression is lacking at this time.*

A few women, typically those with late-onset postpartum depression, can develop a serious condition called "postpartum psychosis." Symptoms of postpartum psychosis include delusions, hallucinations, restlessness, insomnia, confusion, mania, and even suicidal or homicidal ideas. Postpartum psychosis can develop in women with long-standing, untreated postpartum depression. It is a medical emergency. Fortunately, it is rare and only affects about 0.1 to 0.2 percent of women.[25] Although postpartum psychosis is more common in women with preexisting bipolar disease or depression, the risk of hospitalization for these women during the first two months after delivery is many times higher than usual.[26] This suggests that something during, or immediately after, the birth process triggers this condition in biologically vulnerable people.

Treatment for postpartum depression usually depends on the severity of the symptoms. Surprisingly, hormonal treatment has not helped postpartum depression. Many women recover with support and basic counseling. Group therapy helps women feel less isolated and guilty about their condition.[27] Antidepressant medications can be used, but this treatment becomes complicated if the mother is breast-feeding her infant, since the antidepressant can appear in breast milk. Cooperation between different treating specialists is often necessary to optimize the treatment of postpartum depression. With prompt and appropriate therapy, the prognosis for this condition is excellent.

More depressing news

This brief overview of five common causes of depression doesn't come close to completing the list. For example, there are also at least two major types of bipolar disease. Other conditions associated with depression include substance-induced depression, minor or atypical depression, childhood presentations of depression, major depression with schizoaffective disorder, depression associated with neuro-degenerative diseases, like Parkinsonism or Alzheimer's disease, cyclothymic disorder, fibromyalgia, chronic fatigue syndrome, and much more. Some people experience more than one of these forms of depression at one time or another. Moreover, there are many different variations of presentation within each condition.

There is a self-assessment quiz at the back of the book (Appendix C) that may help you delve a little more deeply into the possibility of depression in your life. We want to urge you, however, to seek out the counsel of your medical doctor before embarking on any treatment programs.

I (Rich) will close this chapter with a true story that will illustrate in a personal way how depression can change a person's life. Like almost everyone who suffers from one form of depression or another, the story of Trina is complex. Many avenues of treatment went into her attempts at recovery, but thankfully her story included a happy ending.

Trina's story

"Seven pounds, eight and a half ounces. Twenty-one inches long," the nurse said. Another nurse recorded the newborn's statistics on a clipboard. The delivery room was chaotic with the hustle and bustle of managing a new addition to the world's population.

This was Trina's first child—a healthy baby girl. She and Bob, teenage sweethearts, had been married for three years. Their new baby girl, Jody, was planned from the beginning. The ultrasound told the couple to expect a girl. The baby's room was decked out in pink and bursting with the visual delights of brightly colored toys and cozy teddy bears. All it needed was little Jody to occupy the newly acquired crib.

These were happy times for the couple. Bob was making good money as an investment banker. He and Trina had recently moved into a brand-new home in anticipation of the new little family member. There was money in the bank and proud grandparents in town to celebrate and help with the new arrival. Trina was able to quit her job to be a full-time mom: her dream come true. Everything seemed right with the world—until Trina's life took a sharp turn into the dark.

At first, Trina noticed she was irritable and would weep suddenly for no good reason. She was also experiencing extreme mood and energy swings. Trina tried to adjust to them by planning her life in advance. When she felt well, she would prepare food and freeze it for the days when she felt fatigued. She did her grocery shopping and ran errands on good days. The laundry had to wait for these days too. So did the baby bottles which she prepared in advance for those moments when she had no energy. But there were fewer and fewer good days, and Trina was feeling more edgy and melancholic every day. Before long, one bleak hopeless day followed another until she was sure she'd rather be dead than alive.

Trina couldn't bring herself to believe something was wrong. She was miserable, and she felt like a failure. She felt guilty because she was falling behind in her household chores. She felt ungrateful and unworthy of all her blessings: her home, her loving husband, and her new baby girl. How could everything be so wrong?

Trina made an appointment with her pastor. He immediately recognized the signs of postpartum depression. With this insight, Trina made an appointment with her family doctor, who started her on medication. Both she and Bill met for weekly counseling with a Christian psychologist in her congregation. Trina discovered simple things seemed to help her most early in the course of her illness. Her counselor advised her to set easy goals for herself on her bad days—like just getting out of bed and showering.

The couple agreed to let church friends and family prepare a few meals from time to time and help out with some needed chores. Her physician made an adjustment in her medication. Her pastor advised her to remain faithful in her Bible reading, church attendance, and prayer time. Concerned friends and family prayed for her and with her. All of these things helped Trina cope with her depression. They gave her hope. They added light to her gloom. Finally, the medication was stopped after about nine months of treatment, just in time for Trina to enjoy watching Jody take her first steps! Trina had joy in her life again! The oppressive darkness of her depression was gone.

Eleanor Roosevelt once said, "It is better to light one small candle than to curse the darkness." This is wise advice for anyone with depression. It is also good counsel for anyone who wishes to help someone with depression. Becoming properly equipped to manage depression can help light more than one small candle in someone's life; it can kindle a bonfire of hope that illuminates the journey to full recovery.

chapter 5

Fearfully and Wonderfully Made:

Brain Chemistry and Depression

> Brain: an apparatus with which we think we
> think.
> — AMBROSE BIERCE, AMERICAN AUTHOR AND
> SATIRIST

In the next several chapters, Rich and I will explain how the treatment of depression must be holistic because the illness is comprehensive, involving every component of human nature: our physiology
(the purely physical side of us), our thoughts and emotions, and our
spirituality. It is not fair to suggest treatment or healing from
depression without considering carefully each of these elements of
human life.

In this chapter Dr. Rich explains clearly how the human brain
works and why depression can be rooted in our physiology. He'll
outline steps we can take to make our bodies stronger, and in turn,
make us more whole. Rich also explains in this chapter why antidepressant medications have helped so many people—and why they
don't help everyone. When I (Gary) first read Rich's draft for this

chapter, I was amazed, fascinated, and enriched as I got a glimpse into the mystery and wonder of the human brain.

The Telephone Game

The room erupted in laughter.

"My mother's cradle is full of rocks? Was that the message?" asked Boomer, the last person in the line.

The group was playing the telephone game. To play this game, all of the participants line up so that each can whisper to their immediate neighbor without being overheard by anyone else. The person at the beginning of the line thinks of a phrase and whispers it to the next person. The message is passed down the line, whisper by whisper, until it reaches the last person. Each person listening hears it a little differently, so by the time it comes out the other end of the "telephone line," the sentence or phrase becomes hilariously garbled!

"No!" Beth laughed. "The message I started was, 'The hand that rocks the cradle rules the world.' How did *that* become 'My mother's cradle is full of rocks'?" There were only five people playing the game, but it didn't take many exchanges to mix up the message.

Your brain is like the telephone game, only a *lot* more complicated. *Millions* of nerve cells line up along predetermined routes to "whisper" messages to one another. They also branch off in many directions to define a network we don't fully understand. Thoughts, emotions, sensations, movement, and countless other activities emerge from this wonderful labyrinth of human flesh and electrical impulses. Under the microscope, the "wiring" in your brain looks like a tangled, chaotic mess. Yet your brain is meticulously and miraculously organized to accomplish all the activities of life. There is a "method to the madness." We *are* fearfully and wonderfully made, but because we live in a fallen and imperfect world, things can go wrong.

Your brain is organized around centers of activity. For example, one part of your brain allows you to see the print on this page. An adjacent part helps you understand what you are seeing, while a different part of your brain tells you how to move your eyes to read. Still another allows you to remember what you read. There is even a part of your brain that stirs up emotions and memories associated with what you are reading. These brain centers collaborate and make reading this book possible. While reading, you're also breathing, your heart is beating, you're hearing sounds in the room, you're digesting your last meal, you're filtering impurities out of your blood, and your body is doing dozens of other things you don't even have to think about. All these brain centers are connected by countless nerve bundles speaking to one another.

There's a whole lot of interconnected telephone games going on in your head! But it gets even more complicated. When the nerves in your brain play the telephone game, the messages they whisper are really different chemicals. Each nerve "whispers" a substance to the cell next to it. Each chemical carries a unique message depending on where the nerves are located in your head and what chemicals they release. That's because different sections of your mind are organized to perform unique tasks, and different brain compounds act differently.

Scientists call our brain's chemical messengers "neurotransmitters." One of these neurotransmitters is serotonin (ser-oh-tone-in). This neurotransmitter whispers messages that bring us self-confidence, pain tolerance, and emotional stability. Without it, a person is left with feelings of sadness and remorse, and thoughts of helplessness and hopelessness. Another important neurotransmitter is norepinephrine (nor-ep-in-nef-rin). This chemical messenger communicates energy, arousal, and drive. If there's not enough nor-epinephrine, we experience lethargy, inattention, poor appetite, low libido, and a lack of motivation.

Pulitzer Prize novelist William Styron once said, "The weather of depression is unmodulated; it's like a brownout." This is a good description of depression. When one or more neurotransmitters runs low, nerve cells begin to send weak or even wrong signals to one another. The low chemical messengers dim brain electricity. The nerves playing the telephone game whisper too softly to be heard clearly by their neighbors. Messages get lost or confused. One part of your brain cannot speak to another part clearly. Thoughts and emotions flicker and dim, and the symptoms of depression begin. It's a brain brownout.

Running on Empty

Running low on neurotransmitters can happen in different ways. These chemicals are made by nerve cells and are consumed in the process of thinking, feeling, or acting. All this is under complex genetic control. Normally, there's a balance between making neurotransmitters and consuming them. But when neurotransmitters are used faster than they are made, their levels become critically low. That's when symptoms of depression emerge.

Increased daily demands of life can increase the use of neurotransmitters. For example, when we experience stress in our lives, we use up brain chemicals more vigorously. Even things that we regard to be good or pleasant can overstress the chemical balance in our heads. Marriage, buying a new home, and even inheriting a fortune from Uncle Albert can step up the pace of neurotransmitter use. If we are genetically vulnerable, we may soon find ourselves inexplicably depressed. If we run too fast, we risk running on empty.

One D-myth says that depression is an emotional or mental illness, but the delineation between physical illness and mental illness is artificial. God created us as *whole living beings*. Each of us has a seamlessly integrated body, mind, and spirit. Disease cannot afflict one part of us without distressing the whole person. For example, a serious physical condition is a major stressor that can cause depression. Patients with chronic illnesses like cancer,[1] arthritis,[2] or lupus are at risk for depression.[3] Depression also makes the symptoms of these chronic illnesses worse.[4] The effects can go both ways. While cancer patients often struggle with depression, patients with depression are three times more likely to have a heart attack, develop a serious illness, or even experience sudden death.[5]

A person with depression is physically, spiritually, mentally, socially, and emotionally impaired. But those who have bought into the D-myths expect people with depression to just "shake it off" or carry on like nothing is wrong. Treating depression this way is like walking on a broken leg without a cast. Needless pain, even physical harm, can result. In fact, although mild depression sometimes can pass after many months without treatment, ignoring depression is now known to cause brain damage that proper treatment can prevent.[6] Severe bouts of depression can be life-threatening. It just makes sense to get professional help.

There are some simple things we can do to help ourselves physically, but first we must ensure that we have acquired the right knowledge and developed the skills we need. Here are some of the simple elements that will help build a stronger body.

Balanced Sleep

Our mothers taught us that we need a good night's sleep. As usual, Mom was right. A loss of sleep elevates our blood pressure and heart rate. It increases blood chemical markers for stress, inflammation, and cardiovascular disease.[7] Sleep deprivation also has harmful effects on the immune system. For example, the antibody response to vaccination is blunted after sleep deprivation.[8] A chronic lack of sleep makes us vulnerable to viral and bacterial infections.[9] Other illnesses, such as cancer and arthritis, may also be affected adversely by sleep deprivation. Since we know that physical illness is a risk for depression, it only makes sense to avoid anything that may cause illness.

Sleep deprivation itself may cause depression because *sleep actually restores the normal brain neurotransmitter balance and distribution.*[10] Some neurotransmitter levels rise during the sleeping process,[11] and many doctors believe that the fatigue and sleepiness of depression is the body's way of trying to recover from the illness.

It is tempting to conclude that hours of *extra* sleep are just what the doctor ordered, but here's where the complexity of depression is evident. To advise more sleep could do more harm than good in people who are depressed. Common sense tells us that people who are ill should get lots of rest, but scientific evidence suggests that sleep can be part of the problem with depression. Some forms of depression may actually be sleep disorders, like obstructive sleep apnea or restless leg syndrome. Those people who suffer from depression begin the dreaming stage of sleep very quickly after falling asleep, so the amount of time spent dreaming in patients with depression is excessive compared to those who do not have depression.

Antidepressant medications commonly decrease the percentage of sleep time spent dreaming. In fact, mild sleep deprivation actually improves the symptoms of depression. Missing one night's sleep is the only intervention known that can actually improve depression overnight, although it doesn't work for all people.[12] For reasons mentioned earlier, regularly missing sleep is not recommended. Yet it is wise to limit sleep to no more than seven or eight hours per night. It is best to resist the overpowering desire to sleep for long periods of time when depression strikes.

A proper duration of sleep, then, can help lift the gloom of depression. Scientists have also discovered that a brief exposure to bright light can also improve symptoms of depression. One form of depression has long been known to respond to bright light: Seasonal Affective Disorder (SAD), which I discussed in chapter 4. In northern latitudes, SAD occurs most frequently during winter months. Short days and long nights associated with gray overcast skies cause predisposed individuals to become depressed.

Yet light therapy does not benefit only those with SAD. There is now evidence that exposure to bright light on a daily basis helps some people who have major depression. For example, one study shows that going outdoors between 11:00 A.M. and 2:00 P.M. each day can greatly improve depression. In up to a third of patients with major depression, only thirty minutes of bright sunshine daily causes a significant reduction in melancholic symptoms.[13]

Bright light, rather than any particular type of light, seems to be the key to effective treatment. Several companies make and sell light boxes and other bright light sources designed to help people with depression. With the exception of an afternoon stroll outside, however, it is important to use light therapy under the supervision of a physician.

Aerobics for Your Brain: Exercise

Another simple physical measure that can lighten your mood is exercise. Often, the last thing a depressed person wants to do is jog or attend an aerobics class, but regular exercise does maintain overall health, which is helpful in preventing some depressive episodes. Exercise helps control some of the symptoms associated with depression. For example, regular exercise eases anxiety and agitation that people with depression sometimes experience.

Regular exercise can also help the melancholy of depression, but an occasional stroll around the house is not enough to make a difference. At least thirty minutes of daily exertion, on most days, at a level of intensity required to maintain cardiovascular fitness is required. This can be as simple as walking briskly for a half hour each day. When you do this during the early afternoon, the exercise combines with exposure to bright light to improve the outcome even more.[14]

Helpful Foods

The food we eat can also influence our mood. Neurotransmitters in our brain ultimately come from basic nutrients in our diet. A well-balanced diet is important for good health, but some food sources are more helpful than others when it comes to depression. For example, research suggests that taking fish oil, available without a prescription in various formulations, can improve depression within three to four weeks. This is true even in patients who have not responded well to traditional antidepressant medications.[15] It is vital to consult a physician before taking any over-the-counter medications or food additives.

Avoiding some foods is also important for those with depression. Some people believe the artificial sweetener, Aspartame, can cause medical problems. For example, people with a genetic disease called PKU (phenylketonuria) should avoid Aspartame.[16] Although the FDA believes Aspartame is safe, and much of the scientific literature verifies this, some investigators believe it can cause seizures or migraine headaches in vulnerable people. There is evidence that Aspartame may also block a therapeutic response to antidepressant medication.[17] With this information, it may be prudent to avoid Aspartame if there is a history of depression.

Other substances can also depress the central nervous system. These include alcohol, narcotics, and sedatives. The list of agents with sedating or depressive influences is long and varied. Some cold remedies contain antihistamines that are depressants. Barbiturates, benzodiazepines (like Valium), and sleeping medications are also on this list. In general, we should only take medication, food additives, herbal remedies, or health foods when they are prescribed or approved by a physician who is fully informed about our overall medical condition.

Worts and All

One herbal remedy for depression that has gained considerable attention in recent years is Saint-John's-wort, also known as *Hypericum perforatum*. It comes from a common yellow wild flower, goatweed, which grows in Europe and North America. Available in the United States without a prescription in various formulations, it is widely prescribed and used in Europe to treat mild depression.

Unfortunately, Saint-John's-wort is not regulated by the Food and Drug Administration (FDA), so quality control of some over-the-counter Saint-John's-wort products has been poor. For example, the Good Housekeeping Institute found inconsistent potency in the tablets of a half dozen popular preparations of the herb.[18] An investigation by the *Los Angeles Times* showed a wide variation in pill-to-pill potency in the majority of commercial Saint-John's-wort products.[19]

The effectiveness of Saint-John's-wort in relieving depression is still debated. A large well-controlled study conducted by the National Institutes of Health (NIH) in 2002 showed that Saint-John's-wort was no better than a placebo (sugar pills) in treating depression.[20] Some investigators, though, have questioned the design and conclusions of this study. There is no evidence that Saint-John's-wort is effective in severe depression, but some studies show that it benefits people with mild or moderate depression. No one yet knows how it works.

Saint-John's-wort does have several important effects on the metabolism that we need to be aware of: First, it can interfere with treatment for some life-threatening diseases, like AIDS.[21] Second, those who take "blood thinners" (anticoagulants), such as warfarin, should not take Saint-John's-wort.[22] Third, women who are breast-feeding and people who take other antidepressants should not use Saint-John's-wort.[23] This may be repetitive, but the best advice remains to take Saint-John's-wort *only under the supervision of a physician*.

The simple measures we have mentioned—daily exercise, a nutritious diet, the right amount of sleep, bright light early in the day, and Saint-John's-wort—may help prevent a recurrence of depression. However, in spite of our best efforts and for no apparent "good reason," depression can still occur. When this happens, it is wise to consult a physician quickly to get help. Depression is a downward spiral that only gets worse when not interrupted by treatment. It doesn't just go away by ignoring it or wishing it wasn't there. There is a lot of help available today, coming in many different forms.

We'll now turn to something we've already mentioned in this book—prescribed medications—and look at its role in treating depression in more detail.

Medications

My wife's condition went undiagnosed for a long time before anyone realized she was depressed. When we finally recognized her depression, our family doctor started her on a medication called desipramine, which helped her melancholy within about two weeks. Sue's insomnia continued to be a problem, however, so her doctor added a small dose of a second antidepressant, trazadone, to her regimen at bedtime.

Although Sue's depression and insomnia improved with these drugs, she experienced troublesome lightheadedness when she got up too quickly. The medication also made her drowsy during the day. The side effects became milder with time, but they never completely disappeared. Even when Sue's depression was gone, medication side effects continued to be a problem.

Her doctor reduced the dosages of both medications and finally stopped them after Sue was free from depression for about six months. When her depression recurred about one year later, it was clear to her physician that she needed lifelong treatment with medication. Because of her previous problems with side effects, a newer but more expensive medication—sertraline—was started and adjusted to an effective dose. Sue experienced almost no side effects from the new drug. Now, after more than seven years of continuous antidepressant medication, she remains happy, productive, and whole. Sue was finally on the right treatment for her.

The Nature of Antidepressant Medication

Antidepressant medication is one of the most common and effective forms of depression treatment. As in Sue's case, the medication must be individualized to the needs of each person. Scientists classify antidepressants into different types, depending on their chemical structure and how they work. Each type of antidepressant has its own useful characteristics and side effects. For example, some types of antidepressants work best in patients with atypical forms of depression, while other types should be avoided in elderly patients.

The side effects seen from antidepressant drugs can actually be beneficial. For example, antidepressants with sedating effects are useful in people with anxiety or severe insomnia, while antidepressants with activating side effects help patients with lethargy and fatigue. Choosing the right antidepressant is often an educated guess. Sometimes a little trial and error is needed. It is important not to give up or become discouraged if the first medication is not effective or if the person being treated has undesired side effects.

Not habit-forming or addicting

Antidepressants are *not* addicting or habit forming. No one wants to buy or sell these drugs on the street. They don't make people "high" or cause drug-induced emotions or thoughts. Antidepressant medications do, however, take skill to prescribe and manage properly. For example, most antidepressants should not be stopped abruptly. Tapering the medication dose prior to discontinuation prevents the undesired symptoms that occur if the drug is suddenly stopped. Also, there is a slight increase in the risk of suicide, a common risk in depression anyway, when antidepressant medication treatment is first started. The reason for this is not known, but this risk can be minimized by being aware of it and by taking practical precautions. The treating physician should provide additional information and advice about this to both the patient and the family.

From our earlier discussion you'll recall that antidepressants probably work by changing the levels of effectiveness of one or more neurotransmitters in the brain. For that reason, they are useful in patients with moderate or severe depression. Research shows that 50 to 65 percent of depressed patients will improve after about three months of antidepressant treatment. Some patients require more than one medication before their symptoms improve, and other patients do not respond to medical treatment at all. Obviously, there is still much to learn about depression and its therapy. For readers interested in the fascinating history and development of commonly used antidepressants, please refer to Appendix B in the back of this book.

Next we want to briefly discuss a terribly misunderstood treatment for depression—shock therapy. We feel we must address this at least briefly because of the extraordinary misinformation swirling around about this therapy. Like medication, it is one of the physiological strategies that can be used to treat depression. It is not appropriate for everyone, of course. It is mainly used in severe cases of depression that are not responding to other types of treatment.

Electroconvulsive Therapy

The psychotic depression experienced by Bill after the death of his wife, Marci, (a story we told in chapter 3) is a good example of a case that responds well to electroconvulsive therapy (ECT), sometimes called "shock treatment." Bill was hallucinating, confused, and unresponsive to other forms of treatment so, for him, ECT was life-saving.

Few areas of antidepressant treatment are more stigmatized than ECT. It is the subject of many false ideas and superstition; as a result, many people fear even considering it as a treatment. As I mentioned before, ECT is more effective in treating life-threatening or severe depression than any other known therapy. Somehow, some way, the electrical system of the brain is, in many cases, "reset" by shock therapy.

It is now known that ECT increases brain neurotransmitter levels. It can also stimulate new nerve growth in areas that have become blighted by depression.[24]

ECT is generally reserved for the most severely ill patients. Patients with intractable depression that is unresponsive to medication or psychotherapy often respond well to ECT. Also, patients who are suicidal, homicidal, or manic from their depression have dramatic relief from their symptoms. In fact, suicidal attempts are almost unknown in depressed patients who have begun ECT.

Although ECT should be reserved for only the most severe cases of depression, it is nevertheless a safe and painless therapy. Patients are put to sleep with a short-acting sedative before the treatment is started. An agent that briefly paralyzes the muscles is given to block the jerking action of the induced convulsion. A small, one-second-long electrical current is applied to the head by electrodes attached to the scalp. The patient sleeps through the "internal brain convulsion" that occurs. The patient's electrocardiogram (EKG) and electroencephalogram (EEG) are monitored during therapy. Oxygen is given during the treatment to improve safety even further. The invisible seizures last about thirty seconds.

Patients usually awaken shortly after ECT, feeling slightly groggy and sedated. ECT is usually given several times a week for many weeks, depending on the severity of the illness and how well the patient responds to the treatment. Short-term memory loss is the most common side effect. Patients may experience some decrease in memory for a month or so following ECT. About one half of 1 percent of all patients getting ECT have persistent memory problems. Although the idea of electrically induced seizures is frightening, this treatment should not be avoided when a patient's condition is desperate or failing to improve with other forms of depression treatment.

There are many simple things we can do to face the challenges of depression. In the end, through the fault of no one, these simple things may not be enough. When depression emerges anyway, we need the humility and courage to seek and accept expert help. This help may include prayer, psychotherapy, medication, counseling, the support of friends and family, and even hospitalization. And the odds of complete recovery improve considerably when the *whole* person is treated.

In the next chapter we will examine why treating depression from a strictly physiological (physical) perspective may not hold all the answers we are seeking. The physical aspect of depression is a great starting place and, for some, it may adequately relieve their symptoms. But if you have sought out a physician, taken whatever medication is recommended, but still feel something is wrong, read on. Your approach to treating depression will probably need to address the spiritual and psychological needs that you have as well.

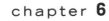

chapter 6

Heaven Help Us!

Biblical Insights Into Depression

*The Lord God formed man of the dust of the ground,
and breathed into his nostrils the breath of life; and
man became a living soul.*
—GENESIS 2:7 KJV

It seems like a simple formula for a human life: one part dirt, mixed
with one part breath of life, and *voilá!* a human soul! Human
beings, however, are more than the sum of their parts. To get the
big picture, we must first understand those parts and how they con-
verge as a whole person.

According to Genesis, God used the good ground of earth to
create human life, and He called the first man Adam because the
Hebrew word for ground is *adamah*. Formed out of the dust of the
ground, Adam was bound to the earth where God placed him. His
five senses allowed him to interact with the physical aspects of his
world, and his remarkable brain allowed him to think, assess,
remember, and communicate. His musculoskeletal system empow-
ered him with movement and the capacity to change his surround-
ings. He was perfect.

Almost.

As God watched him in Eden, he observed that: "It is not good for the man to be alone. I will make a helper suitable for him" (Genesis 2:18). Adam needed the companionship of someone like himself, yet different—a woman. God does not save Adam from his aloneness. *The woman does,* as she becomes his "helpmeet," or "a helper suitable." This is a translation of a Hebrew term, the root of which is used some eighty times in the Old Testament. Generally it means *military assistance,* not exactly a wimpy word!

It makes sense that our God of love (1 John 4:16) would design us with the need and capacity for love. Adam and Eve were of the same essence as this material world. They were physical beings. Therefore, God designed and created them with the ability to express love in physical terms. Their bodies were not the same. They were complementary, suitable both to give and receive intimacy.

God said, "Be fruitful and increase in number" (Genesis 1:28), which means we actually multiply love through procreation. A husband and wife who love their children must meet their physical needs. We show love to other people in a similar way. This give-and-take between people is as vital to our well-being as food, water, and air. So God has placed us in an interdependent relationship with one another and the world around us.

But there's more.

The Breath of God

Apart from the breath of God, Adam's earthy body would be little more than a fleshy castle of sand (Genesis 2:7). Divine breath (Hebrew: *ruach*) was the life-force that made Adam a living, sentient being. Without the spirit (God's breath), our body returns to the dust from which it came (Ecclesiastes 12:7; Job 34:14–15).

Just as our physical bodies invest us with physical abilities and needs, our spirits empower us with spiritual abilities and needs. Prayer, worship, and praise are spiritual functions. The apostle John wrote, "God is spirit, and those who worship Him must worship in spirit and truth" (John 4:24 NASB). Our spirit, or spiritual capacity, allows us to know God and to know right from wrong without the benefit of instruction or experience (Romans 1:18–20). Insight and revelation come to us from the spiritual realm, bathing our inner life with the very life of God, yet we have no way to detect this scientifically.

Indeed, many experts differentiate between the brain, as a physical function of the human body, and the mind, that mysterious and elusive spiritual side of every person's nature. Remarkably, some people have had "near death experiences," where they "see" themselves leaving their body, even though all other life functions—including electrical activity in the brain—have ceased. "Brain-dead" people have "returned" from the other side of death!

Sometimes called *intuition,* spiritual knowing is real and vital to our well-being if it is coming from our creator God. As the physical body is our means of being world-conscious, so the spirit is our means of being conscious of God. The result is that we live in two realms: the physical and the spiritual. For example, love is more than physical procreation or material generosity. Loving others has a spiritual, transcendent dimension as well. This aspect of human caring, rooted in the spiritual part of our soul, endows love with nobility, integrity, and humility.

Our empirical and scientific culture often ignores the spiritual aspect of the human soul. To understand fully who we are, we must acknowledge both the eternal as well as the earthly elements of our lives. Yet understanding these two dimensions alone still is not enough.

One Plus One Equals Three

The *ruach* (breath) of God gives our physical body *life*. Yet one part spirit and one part body produces more than two interactive elements of human nature. Wondrous and complex human life emerges from the synergy of spirit and flesh. Consider Genesis 2:7 again: "The Lord God formed the man from the dust of the ground and breathed into his nostrils the breath of life, *and the man became a living being*." As "living souls," we are capable of deep thoughts and emotions. Our mind is something more than electrical impulses. Often referred in the Bible as "the heart," our mind transcends the remarkable chemistry of the brain. We have a will and make choices. We become responsible moral agents who must conscientiously live in physical and spiritual realms.

In addition to physical and spiritual needs, each person has complex "soulish" needs. For example, people have a need for significance and security. These needs, when met, give us a sense of personal worth necessary for health and well-being.[1] They are keys to our identity. They are the reasons we seek hobbies, engage in creative activities, and need social interaction.

It's interesting that both the Hebrew (*nephesh*) and Greek (*psuche*) words for "soul" can also be translated "living being." These original languages of the Bible recognize the seamless integration of spirit/soul/body into a single person. If our body gives us world-consciousness and our spirit gives us God-consciousness, then our soul gives us self-consciousness.

As we've already said, depression blights the whole person: spirit, soul, and body. Note how in contrast to depression, the "God of peace" wants to make you whole: "May God himself, the God of peace, sanctify you through and through. May your whole spirit, soul and body be kept blameless at the coming of our Lord Jesus Christ" (1 Thessalonians 5:23). In contrast to the God of peace, depression rapes our "living being." To understand this more, let's reflect on how the soul of man, created in perfection, fell into corruption and disease.

Paradise Lost

The golden orb edged above the eastern horizon. As the lush grass hung gray-green in a heavy mist, fantastic new life-forms stirred in the dawn of Paradise. The earth warmed to a new day as a gentle breeze whispered the name of God. It was, indeed, a perfect time for a walk in a perfect garden.

Carefree yet full of purposeful life, the woman danced in the scent of luxuriant ferns and flowering trees. Deep in emerald Eden she heard the resonant voice of a beautiful, terrible creature asking her softly, "Did God *really* say, 'You must not eat from any tree in the garden'?"

The morning light shimmered like gemstones on the serpent's scales: cobalt, lavender, crimson, and gold. Radiating with cynical confidence, he held his narrow head high as he awaited the woman's answer.

"We may eat fruit from the trees in the garden, but God did say, 'You must not eat fruit from the tree that is in the middle of the garden, and you must not touch it, or you will die,'" the woman said.

A sneer played in the corner of his mouth: "You will not surely die, for God knows that when you eat of it your eyes will be opened, and you will be like God, knowing good and evil" (Genesis 3:1–4).

She froze as their eyes met. Without turning her head, she looked quickly right, then left. Was someone watching? Then, as if in a trance, the woman offered the serpent her unblemished hand.

She felt the fruit, cool and firm, as she brought it slowly to her mouth.

And she ate.

Her lover was nearby. With a look on her face he had never seen, she offered the fruit to him. He too froze in her gaze, and as he ate he had the sensation he was falling to his death from the highest tree in the garden. As quickly as God had said not so long ago, "It is good," Adam and Eve fell from Paradise, and human life has never been the same.

Whatever you may think about our fanciful retelling of this ancient narrative, few would deny that there is something terribly wrong with human nature. There's a side to us as dark as the far side of the moon. Christians believe that the innocent faith of our first parents could not withstand the suspicions the serpent raised about God. Their trust and faith in their creator God imploded in doubt and disobedience. The result of their fall into sin was a radical transformation of their essential natures. Everything looked different to them. Nothing was quite so comfortable or trustworthy. Adam and Eve experienced new sensations: fear, doubt, confusion, and shame. They hid from God and covered themselves with fig leaves, mankind's first attempts at self-salvation. But fig leaves couldn't atone for their disbelief and rebellion or undo the damage in their souls.

Our Collective Fall

Adam and Eve's sin had a devastating and lasting effect on every human life after them. The blessing of conception and procreation morphed into the pains of childbirth—and all the suffering inherent in raising children (Genesis 3:16). Furthermore, the Lord cursed the very ground from which He made us (Genesis 3:17–19). As a result, now it only yields its bounty through thorns, thistles, and the sweat of Adam's brow.

Think about it! The essential building blocks of our bodies, our basic biochemistry, come from that condemned ground: carbon, trace metals, phosphorus, and other elements from the earth, which wondrously assemble themselves in a mother's womb to form a child. In a very real sense, every living cell is bound by the curse of God on the ground, on *adamah*. As we have already discussed in this book, there are very often physical (physiological) reasons for depression. Perhaps we could say that the physical causes of depression are "thorns and thistles" in the *adamah* of our bodies.

It should not surprise us, then, that depression from bodily defects can cause emotional and mental problems. Recall that the melding of body and spirit produces a living soul, a person capable of thoughts, emotions, and choices. Any physiological, anatomical, or biochemical malady disrupts the entire person. Diseases we do not usually regard as emotional or mental illnesses—like heart attacks, cancer, and arthritis—can actually cause depression, and when depression occurs, it increases our risk for other "physical" illnesses.

Since the soul has spiritual dimensions, depression can have spiritual causes as well. For example, spiritual neglect can make us *vulnerable to depression*. When Christians disregard the care and feeding of their spiritual lives, they can become discouraged, even depressed. A neglect of Bible study, prayer, praise, worship, and church fellowship takes its toll. Pastor and author Dr. Douglas Rumford calls this "soul neglect."[2]

Spiritual giants, like Elijah, who were diligent in their walk with God and faithful to His word, became depressed when they were exhausted and emotionally distressed. After his encounter with the prophets of Baal—and the demons they represented—Elijah proclaimed in despair, "I have had enough, Lord. Take my life; I am no better than my ancestors" (1 Kings 19:4). Elijah's distorted perception of his situation and his longing to die are typical for clinical depression. Our spiritual condition can render us vulnerable to disease and spiritual attack.

In Elijah's case, God ministered to his whole person: body, soul, and spirit. The Lord sent an angel to encourage Elijah to eat, drink, and sleep. Yet food and rest alone were not enough to revive Elijah. They could not meet his spiritual needs. The angel also "touched" Elijah twice as he ministered to him (1 Kings 19:5–9). The Hebrew word *naga,* translated "touch" in the NIV, could also be rendered "lay the hand upon."[3] This laying on of hands was a common means of spiritual ministry in the Bible (Acts 8:18; 1 Timothy 4:14), and recent research is rediscovering the healing power of compassionate human touch.[4] Additionally, God's loving attention to Elijah affirmed his value and significance. We see in Elijah's case that God met every human need he had in body, soul, and spirit. He would not have fully recovered if any one of these components had not been addressed.

For those suffering with depression, it is important to know the spiritual resources we have for treatment. Since we are spiritual beings, there are pathways we can take that will help to restore balance to our souls and thereby reduce our suffering from depression. Following, we will look at four pathways that hold great potential for our well-being.

Spiritual Pathways to Healing

Pathway 1: Get in step with God.

The first step to spiritual wholeness is making sure you have a personal relationship with God. From Scripture we know that the way we enter into relationship with our creator God is through inviting

Jesus Christ—His Son—into our hearts and then living our lives as devoted followers of Him. It is not trying to "be good" or to engage in merely outward religious exercises. Rather, it is a trust in God himself to provide what we need to live godly lives.

I was interviewed recently by a journalist who was still asking questions about why church attendance skyrocketed four years ago, after 9/11. For us, church attendance doubled that first weekend after the attack on New York and Washington, but within three or four weeks we were back to "normal." Why, the journalist wondered, did such an extraordinary national catastrophe not have a lasting spiritual impact on Americans? I told her, "It is because we have so many other things to distract us. We are *godless*. And by that, I don't simply mean that we don't want the Ten Commandments on public buildings. Rather, we are godless because we live so much of our lives without a second thought about God."

Listen what happens when we leave God out of our lives.

> . . . you will find no repose, no resting place for the sole of your foot. There the Lord will give you an anxious mind, eyes weary with longing, and a despairing heart. You will live in constant suspense, filled with dread both night and day, never sure of your life. In the morning you will say, "If only it were evening!" and in the evening, "If only it were morning!" (Deuteronomy 28:65–67).

The glorious option is to make a conscious effort to keep God first in everything: "The fear of the Lord is the beginning of wisdom, and knowledge of the Holy One is understanding" (Proverbs 9:10).

Pathway 2: Shine the light of God's Word into your darkness.

For the person suffering from depression, studying or reading the Bible may seem like an overwhelming, even threatening, task. One of the underlying themes of this book is that severe depression is a highly complex problem, and one D-myth is: "All you have to do is pray and read your Bible."

Because Scripture is alive with the breath of God (2 Timothy 3:16), it does have transforming power, but I must confess there are times *I don't want* to read the Bible; I don't want to hear what it has to say. That's not because I'm mean-spirited about God; it's just that I may doubt whether reading the Bible will actually help me. (Yes, sometimes even big-shot pastors feel that way, but most of them won't admit it.)

On the other hand, when I turn away from darkness and begin reading the Bible, I experience extraordinary healing and renewal. Why? Because the Bible isn't just another self-help book filled with good ideas on how to live my life. It is alive with the presence of God. The Bible has intrinsic power, because God himself comes to us through His Word.

Following are some Bible passages that have comforted me in my dark moments. Read them. Think about them. Have someone else read them to you if you like (a good option if they can do so without lecturing you about how you should do this or that to get un-depressed). Listen to the psalmist talking to himself, speaking to his soul. Then use the Bible to speak into the deep places of your inner being.

> The psalmist says: My tears have been my food day and night, while men say to me all day long, "Where is your God?" ... Why are you downcast, O my soul? Why so disturbed within me? Put your hope in God, for I will yet praise him, my Savior and my God. My soul is downcast within me; therefore I will remember you ... I say to God my Rock, "Why have you forgotten me? Why must I go about mourning, oppressed by the enemy?" My bones suffer mortal agony as my foes taunt me, saying to me all day long, "Where is your God?" Why are you downcast, O my soul? Why so

disturbed within me? [Self-talk] Put your hope in God, for I will yet praise him, my Savior and my God. (Selections from Psalm 42)

The psalmist pleads: "Be merciful to me, Lord, for I am faint; O Lord, heal me, for my bones are in agony. My soul is in anguish. How long, O Lord, how long? Turn, O Lord, and deliver me; save me because of your unfailing love." (Psalm 6:2–4).

I will be glad and rejoice in your love, for you saw my affliction and knew the anguish of my soul. (Psalm 31:7)

For we do not have a high priest who is unable to sympathize with our weaknesses, but we have one who has been tempted in every way, just as we are—yet was without sin. Let us then approach the throne of grace with confidence, so that we may receive mercy and find grace to help us in our time of need. (Hebrews 4:15–16)

[God says]: Fear not, for I have redeemed you; I have summoned you by name; you are mine. When you pass through the waters, I will be with you; and when you pass through the rivers, they will not sweep over you. When you walk through the fire, you will not be burned; the flames will not set you ablaze. (Isaiah 43:1–2)

[Jesus says]: Peace I leave with you; my peace I give you. I do not give to you as the world gives. Do not let your hearts be troubled and do not be afraid. (John 14:27)

Pathway 3: Pray.

Okay, you're depressed. And you're certain your prayers just bounce off the ceiling and never reach God. Maybe you feel like you aren't wording them well, or that you have to *feel* like praying. What to do?

I suppose I should begin by debunking a myth about prayer that goes something like this: *You have to pray a certain way for your prayers to be answered.* For example, people have asked me, "I've heard you are supposed to pray to the Father, in the name of Jesus, and in the power of the Holy Spirit. I've been wanting to talk directly to the Holy Spirit . . . is that okay?"

I've answered this way: *"What? You pray directly to the Holy Spirit? God could never figure that one out!"* Just kidding, of course. But people really ask questions like that because we've made the Christian faith so complicated. We believe we're saved by grace, but after that it's back on the treadmill. We're afraid that God is just waiting for some reason to reject us and not answer our prayer.

No, prayer doesn't work that way. Prayer works *any* way you think you can get through to God under the inspiration of the Holy Spirit. Look at this verse: "Pray in the Spirit on all occasions with all kinds of prayers and requests" (Ephesians 6:18). In Revelation 8:3–4, we read about an "angel, who had a golden censer . . . He was given much incense to offer, with the prayers of all the saints . . . The smoke of the incense, together with the prayers of the saints, went up before God from the angel's hand."

This incense is a symbol of the sacrificial work of Christ, which is a sweet aroma to God. It tells me that *our prayers are deodorized by the sacrifice of Christ.* Our Advocate, Jesus, listens carefully to our prayers and edits them before they get to the Father. I can hear Jesus saying, "My Father, your child has just prayed. It's not a very clearheaded prayer, but I know her heart, and this is what she means."

This is in line with what we read about the intercessory work of the Holy Spirit:

> The Spirit helps us in our weakness. *We do not know what we ought to pray for*, but the Spirit himself intercedes for us . . . in accordance with God's will . . . [which is why] we know that in all

things God works for the good of those who love him, who have been called according to his purpose. (Romans 8:26–28, emphasis mine)

Now that you realize you don't have to pray perfect prayers, that Jesus makes your prayers perfect like every other imperfect thing in your life, notice how prayer is linked directly to receiving the peace of God into your life:

Don't fret or worry. Instead of worrying, pray. Let petitions and praises shape your worries into prayers, letting God know your concerns. Before you know it, a sense of God's wholeness, everything coming together for good, will come and settle you down. It's wonderful what happens when Christ displaces worry at the center of your life. (Philippians 4:6–7 THE MESSAGE)

Pathway 4: Actively engage in spiritual warfare.

I've done extensive study and writing on the subject of spiritual warfare, and I've concluded that our minds interface daily with the spiritual realm. Whether or not you believe it, whether or not you think about it consciously, it's a matter of fact that you have ears to hear and eyes to see something of what is on the other side of time and space. Created in the image of God, humans have a deep spiritual capacity. The chemistry of the human brain is more than chemicals. You can connect with God. And angels.

And the devil?

Paul warns us about this: "I am afraid that just as Eve was deceived by the serpent's cunning, your minds may somehow be led astray from your sincere and pure devotion to Christ" (2 Corinthians 11:3). This is the war zone in your head, and it's why Paul commands Christians to put on the full armor of God, including the helmet of salvation for your head, because "our struggle is not against flesh and blood, but against the rulers, against the authorities, against the powers of this dark world and against the spiritual forces of evil in the heavenly realms" (Ephesians 6:12).

What you think is not always your thoughts. Sometimes it's a power encounter with evil, and the real presence of God is necessary to protect your mind and empower you to believe and obey the Word of God. This brings us to our total dependence on the Holy Spirit, who is the Third Person of God himself. Jesus promised: "I will ask the Father, and he will give you another Counselor to be with you forever—the Spirit of truth" (John 14:16–17). He was speaking of the Holy Spirit, who would take up residence in us when we receive Christ Jesus as our Lord and Savior.

We need divine power, the power of the Holy Spirit, to confront the power of darkness. Our struggles in life are not just with "flesh and blood," but with the devil himself, who "prowls around like a roaring lion looking for someone to devour" (Ephesians 6:11 and 1 Peter 5:8). Sometimes hell's demons act more like jackals or vultures, feeding primarily on weakened prey.

It's typical for spiritual darkness to attack us when we are most vulnerable from battling fatigue, illness, grief, or disappointment. So people suffering from depression are often ripe for demonic attack. The illness saps them of energy, disrupts their sleep, and compromises their ability to concentrate and think clearly. It's at times like these that demons like to whisper into our souls. Christians are not immune either. Rich found this out firsthand, as he and Sue battled the kingdom of darkness. Here's his account of what happened.

It was a bright, sunny day. My wife, Sue, had been free from depression for several months, but she was still taking her medication. Coming home early from the office to surprise her, I was the one surprised. *Sue was in bed, fast asleep, in the middle of the day.* Because of her history of depression, I was immediately alarmed.

"Are you okay?" I asked her.

"I don't feel well," she responded. "I think the depression has returned. I was feeling fine until my old thoughts of worthlessness and suicide flew back into my head." As depression fell on her like a dark and heavy theater curtain, Sue retreated to her bedroom.

Medical schools prepare physicians to take care of the physical and mental concerns of patients, but quite frankly, they do not do well addressing the spiritual needs of patients. As a Christian, however, it was clear to me that, although Sue's problem was primarily physiological, we were also encountering spiritual power of the dark kind.

Then and there, at her bedside, we prayed together for God's help and deliverance, and the "depression" left as quickly as it had come! As we thanked God for this deliverance, I felt as if the Holy Spirit spoke to me: "Your beloved Sue has had a dialogue with a demon." I got the strong sense that it was vital for me to warn her not to do this again!

"Sue, where do you think these thoughts of worthlessness and suicide are coming from?" I asked her.

"I haven't thought about that," she said softly. "I really didn't know."

"Do you like these thoughts?" I persisted. She shook her head, no.

I almost shouted: "Then these thoughts are not coming from you! What about God? Do you think He's giving you these thoughts?"

A smile spread across her face, and I saw a light in her eyes. Sue knew that wasn't true!

"By a process of elimination, then, where do you think these thoughts are coming from?" I asked her, but it felt as if I were asking myself the same question. Looking deeply into her eyes, I said firmly, "This is spiritual warfare."

During the time of my wife's physical depression, she became vulnerable to spiritual attack. The result was that she felt absolutely miserable. She didn't have the energy to perform her daily duties. She felt isolated and alone because she didn't have the emotional or mental capacity to engage in meaningful social activities. She felt like she was abandoning her husband and children as she retreated to her bed to escape her depression.

All that Satan and his agents of darkness had to do was implant in her mind that her negative feelings about herself were true: Her husband didn't love her anymore, and worse, God didn't either. The dark messages in her mind were relentless, and Sue unwittingly engaged them in what I have come to call "demonic dialogue." Demonic attacks are vicious but often subtle. Lurking just beyond the visible world, these menacing, unseen beings are poised to attack the truth with their filthy lies.

When we realized this, the antidote for their "sickness" became apparent to us: pierce every dark lie with the light saber of truth. The apostle Paul wrote, "We do not wage war as the world does . . . We take captive every thought to make it obedient to Christ" (2 Corinthians 10:3, 5). The Holy Spirit gave us the last part of this passage to resist and defeat the demonic thoughts ensnaring Sue's mind. This took discipline. Sue had to practice *rejecting* demonic talk, which was a change from before when she had passively submitted to the negative thoughts she believed to be her own.

Sue had to determine to crowd out the dark thoughts with God's thoughts: that God loved her and had a wonderful plan for her life. The outcome of this spiritual therapy was extraordinary! After some persistent effort in taking every thought captive and making it obedient to Christ, the demonic attacks ceased entirely. Medication *and* God's Word have set Sue free from her depression.

We believe "if the Son sets you free, you will be free indeed" (John 8:36).

In medical school I was taught that ideas of worthlessness and suicidal thoughts were important in making the diagnosis of depression. So we were hesitant about making that diagnosis without such thoughts being present. I've come to believe, however, that these ruminations are not essentially part of the disease itself. Instead, the vulnerable condition of the depressed person makes them a target for demonic oppression. As a result of this insight, I have been able to help many other Christians with depression get free of the terrible scourge of dark thoughts.

Sue's story is a sobering reminder that depression hits us from many angles. Since we are not totally and exclusively physical beings, we must be aware of the spiritual and emotional issues surrounding this disease. Probably the most important thing to remember is that God is the Fountainhead of life, and depression in part is due to our fallenness and alienation from Him as our source of life. That's why a comprehensive model for understanding and treating depression cannot exclude the God-factor.

In the next chapter we will take a look at something else that has helped me (Gary) tremendously in my ongoing struggle with depression: discovering the power of God's grace for the present moment. I pray it will help you too.

chapter 7

Present Grace:

Adopting a Lifestyle of Letting Go

This is the [very] day *the Lord has made; let us rejoice and be glad in it.*
—Psalm 118:24, EMPHASIS MINE

Real life takes place in the here and now. God is always in the moment,
be that moment hard or easy, joyful or painful.
—Henri Nouwen

Major clinical depression is a disease of the "oppressive present"—we feel like we have no future. The present misery is so dominating that tomorrow moves beyond hope. When we are clinically depressed, only the pains of yesterday accompany our excruciating present, because they confirm today's empty worthlessness. People who are clinically depressed want to escape their miserable present, but at times they are simply incapable of rejoicing and being glad, thinking positively, or receiving grace.

Yet the story of grace and God's daily provision must be told. What we have to offer you in this chapter is a significant component of wholeness. If you can't immerse yourself in present grace, at least take baby steps. Read Scriptures about God's love obediently, even if you don't "feel" like it. Or have someone read them to you. Rich and I believe that even a tiny ray of light in your darkness can make a difference. A single match can light an entire room.

When you're depressed, you may not feel worthy of a free gift. You may not think God's grace is for you, but I have good news! You are the very reason why God gives grace. It's ". . . the tender mercy of our God, by which the rising sun will come to us from heaven to shine on those living in darkness and in the shadow of death, to guide our feet into the path of peace" (Luke 1:78–79). *Grace is for those who feel they least deserve it, like those of us who have carried the dark curse of depression.*

Grace is my life message. Sometimes I (Gary) wonder why. I was raised in a Christian home, and I'm a fourth generation pastor. I've never been a terrible sinner like, let's say, the woman who came to Jesus and who, tumbling to the ground before Him, bathed His feet with perfume and dried them with her hair. Luke reports:

> When a woman who had lived a sinful life in that town learned that Jesus was eating at the Pharisee's house, she brought an alabaster jar of perfume, and as she stood behind him at his feet weeping, she began to wet his feet with her tears. Then she wiped them with her hair, kissed them and poured perfume on them. (Luke 7:37–38)

This had to be a terribly awkward moment. I can only imagine if a woman did that to me in the lobby of our church between services on Sunday morning. Especially if she were noticeably attractive and had a job, let's say, working in a strip club. Does the thought of that make you feel a sense of discomfort? Well, you're not alone:

> When the Pharisee who had invited him saw this, he said to himself, "If this man were a prophet, he would know who is touching him and what kind of woman she is—that she is a sinner" (Luke 7:39).

Jesus knew what he was thinking and realized it was a golden moment to talk about why God loves certain people—and why they love Him.

> Jesus answered him, "Simon, I have something to tell you." "Tell me, teacher," he said. "Two men owed money to a certain money-lender. One owed him five hundred denarii, and the other fifty. Neither of them had the money to pay him back, so he canceled the debts of both. Now which of them will love him more?" Simon replied, "I suppose the one who had the bigger debt canceled." "You have judged correctly," Jesus said . . . "I tell you her many sins have been forgiven—for she loved much. But he who has been forgiven little loves little" (Luke 7:40–43, 47).

Me and the Pharisee

I guess I'm like Simon the Pharisee in that basically I'm a pretty good guy. I *could* think: It hasn't been as difficult for God to forgive me as it has been for Him to forgive people like the woman who came to Jesus. *But I don't think that way.* I've never thought that way. Truthfully, I feel a lot like the apostle Paul—another Pharisee: all the good stuff I've done is dog dung compared with knowing Christ.

Like so many other people who have suffered with depression, I have no confidence in my relationship with God based on my "good" life. In fact, sometimes I am so troubled in my soul that I've struggled deeply and painfully with my sense of self-worth. I've told friends that my success is exceeded only by my insecurity. My expectations for myself are always a couple of days ahead of whatever I accomplish today.

This piles on the clinical elements of my depression—and why I am so desperate for the grace of God. Not because I've had so much sin in my life, but because I have so much *stress* in my soul. Because

I'm hard on myself, I assume wrongly that God must be even
harder on me, which is why the message of grace in Paul's writings
is so totally liberating for me.

Was Saint Paul Clinically Depressed?

Type A people who are ambitious, competitive, hard-driving, impa-
tient, and sometimes hostile have high expectations of themselves
and others, but they don't have a corner on depression. Like hurri-
cane Katrina on the Gulf Coast in 2005, depression doesn't look for
particular personality types to strike. It hurts everybody. Yet I'm certain that my personality profile is like many who will read this
book.

I've been a lifelong student of the apostle Paul. I wrote a brief
commentary on Acts for the *Spirit-Filled Life Study Bible* (Thomas
Nelson), and, like Martin Luther, my favorite portions of the Bible
are Romans and Galatians, which present the great Christian doc-
trine of salvation by grace alone. Studying his letters and observing
his life in the book of Acts, I've concluded that Paul was a tortured
type A personality also. He was . . .

- Ambitious, driven: He made three extensive and aggressive
  missionary journeys, and you can feel his irrepressible energies
  in a passage like this: "Forgetting what is behind and straining
  toward what is ahead, I press on toward the goal to win the
  prize" (Philippians 3:13–14).
- Highly educated: "Festus interrupted Paul's defense. 'You are
  out of your mind, Paul!' he shouted. 'Your great learning is
  driving you insane'" (Acts 26:24).
- Competitive: "Do you not know that in a race all the runners
  run, but only one gets the prize? Run in such a way as to get
  the prize" (1 Corinthians 9:24).

- Demanding of himself: "... as for legalistic righteousness, fault-less" (Philippians 3:6).
- Demanding of others: "Barnabas wanted to take John, also called Mark, with them, but Paul did not think it wise to take him, because he had deserted them in Pamphylia and had not continued with them in the work" (Acts 15:37–38).
- Insecure: "I came to you in weakness and fear, and with much trembling" (1 Corinthians 2:3).
- Confrontational and angry: "When Peter came to Antioch, I opposed him to his face, because he was clearly in the wrong" (Galatians 2:11). "Then Paul said to him [the High Priest], 'God will strike you, you whitewashed wall! You sit there to judge me according to the law, yet you yourself violate the law by commanding that I be struck!' Those who were standing near Paul said, 'You dare to insult God's high priest?'" (Acts 23:3–4).

And depressed: Consider one of Paul's more familiar statements: "To keep me from becoming conceited because of these surpassingly great revelations, there was given me a thorn in my flesh, a messenger of Satan, to torment me" (2 Corinthians 12:7). Scholars have debated the precise nature of Paul's "thorn in the flesh." Most have taken the expression literally, assuming that Paul had a physical ailment in his body, perhaps an eye problem, because in Galatians he says he penned the epistle with "large letters" (Galatians 6:11). No literalist, however, thinks Paul's thorn was an actual splinter embedded in his foot or hand. So the meaning of the "thorn" is probably something broader and deeper, which Paul suggests when he adds, "a messenger of Satan, *to torment me*" (literally "to strike me with his fist").

Somehow, hell was pounding on Paul. Both John Calvin and

Martin Luther—who suffered deeply from depression—as well as others have believed Paul's thorn refers to the fiery darts of Satan[1] piercing his soul. This is my view too, with an update: Paul, not able to speak of depression in clinical terms familiar to us today, would likely have thought of his soul-pain as spiritual oppression, a direct hit from the devil. In view of Paul's personality type, however, it's possible that Paul, like other men of genius, was clinically depressed.[2]

I'm not suggesting we overlook the reality that Paul was, indeed, spiritually oppressed. Rich and I both believe that severely depressed people are vulnerable to the dark side of the spiritual realm. We don't believe that depression is *caused* by a demon presence, but depression seems to engage us in some way in spiritual conflict. Even if a person doesn't believe in a real devil, depression feels like hell: dark, mean, lonely, empty, demon-like.

Did the apostle Paul suffer with depression? He certainly had the personality profile for it, and how better could he describe what today would be called clinical depression than: "a messenger from Satan sent to torment me"? *The New Testament in Modern Speech* calls Paul's torment "the agony of impalement, Satan's angel dealing blow after blow."[3]

No one knows with certainty what Paul meant by his "thorn," and many explanations have been offered. It could have been lust, pride, fear, doubt. Some have even suggested is was an ex-wife and/or his divorce from her, as Paul refers to his singleness, yet we know that men in his position in the religious community were nearly always married. In any case, we can't prove that Paul's thorn was, in fact, depression, but it seems as reasonable as any other explanation.

How Paul "Treated" His Pain

No one will ever know with certainty what caused Paul pain. Perhaps that's an unintentional lesson because, as I heard John Maxwell say years ago, "It's not what happens *to* you; it's what happens *in* you." Many things can cause or contribute to depression, like a major loss, a stroke, a chemical imbalance, stress. Even demons? It's seldom helpful to dwell on the common and more comfortable question: *How did I get here?* It's much more helpful, even necessary, to answer a second question: *Where do I go from here?* Let's learn from Paul by observing carefully what he does in response to his pain, identifying his pathways to wholeness.

> To keep me from becoming conceited because of these surpassingly great revelations, there was given me a thorn in my flesh, a messenger of Satan, to torment me. Three times I pleaded with the Lord to take it away from me. But he said to me, "My grace is sufficient for you, for my power is made perfect in weakness" (2 Corinthians 12:7–8).

First, he begs God to deal with the problem: "Three times I pleaded with the Lord to take it away from me." Second, he has to face not only the pain but also God's silence about the pain. Third, he hears what all of us need to hear in our desperate moments: "[God] said to me, *'My grace is sufficient for you,* for my power is made perfect in weakness.'" What does that mean—God's grace is sufficient? When I have nothing, God does nothing? That's supposed to help me?

It has. It does. It will.

I realize this sounds silly, but next to the medication I've taken to increase my serotonin levels, my only hope during my depression has been God's grace. In fact, before I ever knew about the problems with my brain chemistry, God's grace was a very real help in my life.

Paul's Boast

Paul's experience and view of life were quite different from what we hear from the world: "Therefore I will boast all the more gladly about my weaknesses, so that Christ's power may rest on me. That is why, for Christ's sake, I delight in weaknesses, in insults, in hardships, in persecutions, in difficulties. For when I am weak, then I am strong" (2 Corinthians 12:9–10). To Paul, his weaknesses were priceless. Really think about this: He *delighted* in insults, hardships, and difficulties because they put him in a place of utter dependence on God.

My impossibility is God's opportunity.

This is grace.

If God helps those who help themselves, if we have some part to play, if somehow it's up to us, if we have to meet God halfway or partway, *it isn't grace*. Much of the advice Christians give people who are depressed—unless it's grace-based—is counterproductive because "doing something about your depression" assumes you can and should. In fact, just about everything in life assumes that *if* you do *this* then *that* will happen, and if you don't do *that*, *this* will happen. It's the law of cause and effect, and people believe it applies to our relationship with God.

Yet Paul wrote, "'Abraham believed God, and it was credited to him as righteousness.' Now when a man works, his wages are not credited to him as a gift, but as an obligation" (Romans 4:3–4). *Obligation* . . . the very word sounds unpleasant. It's performance orientation. The curse of the law. It's no wonder people who suffer with depression feel so hopeless; they of all people feel little or no self-worth. Yet Paul, instead of finding meaning in self-worth, threw his future back on God. He found his worth in God: "I have been crucified with Christ and I no longer live, but Christ lives in me. The life I live in the body, I live by faith in the Son of God, who loved me and gave himself for me" (Galatians 2:20).

Falling From Grace

I've taught God's unconditional grace for decades. Everyone in our church knows this little phrase: *Jesus plus nothing!* My relationship with God is based on Jesus plus nothing. Grace is my life message, but most of this year I was drifting. My performance-oriented personality was driving me away from the grace of God to the brink of an emotional collapse. I was falling from grace, not because I had committed some terrible sin, but because I was taking on life by myself, which is precisely what Paul meant by "falling from grace": "You who are trying to be justified by law [that is, by your own human effort] have been alienated from Christ; *you have fallen away from grace*" (Galatians 5:4, emphasis mine). Let me tell you how I fell from grace—and how in my weakness I've rediscovered the grace of God.

Last summer I took a sabbatical, my first in thirty-four years of ministry. Yeah, now you see how crazy I am. A friend of mine, Dr. Dan Spaite, head of the department of emergency medicine at the University of Arizona and author of the book *Time Bomb in the Church*, likes to say, "God is going to get His Sabbath one way or another. If you don't take time off to rest and refresh, God will give you that time in a hospital."

Well, like I told you in chapter 2, I was taken to the hospital in an ambulance in May. And then my back went out; I've been to a pain clinic for three cortisone injections in my spine. Earlier this year I had some terrible misunderstandings with some of my best friends and, unrelated to that, my executive pastor and colleague for the last eighteen years resigned. Then my oldest son was told he might have ALS, aka Lou Gehrig's disease, a devastating, life-ending disease. I cried with David on the phone as he told me how he wanted me to take care of his wife and three small children.

Gratefully, it wasn't what the doctor thought, and he's fine now.

But there's more: In June someone on my pastoral staff was arrested, and it was on all the local media outlets. I knew I was out of gas when I started yelling at people on my staff. At a gathering with some of my best friends in ministry (I'm in a covenant group with five other pastors), I told them I had never been so discouraged. They warned me, "If you don't take time off, you're going to crash."

"I can't take time off," I objected. I was thinking to myself, *The church needs me right now*. God *needs me right now*. I knew this was distorted thinking, but I couldn't shake my sense that I was indispensable. I also knew that little proverb: If your five best friends tell you you're drunk, give them the keys!

So I took about six weeks, exactly forty days, to back off. I had my assistant intercept *all* my mail, emails, and phone calls. I had *no* contact with the church during this time. I rested . . . both at home and places away. I enjoyed my family. And I sought God (off and on, I must admit) about my life, the church, and the future. I wanted God to say something profound, something deep, something *specific*. I wanted to come back and tell my church what God had told me. You see, I wanted to *accomplish something* on my sabbatical. I wanted it to be *productive* so I could satisfy my type A personality. Moses spent forty days with God, and he came away from that time with a list of ten specific things. I wanted God to also give me and our church a to-do list.

Nothing Is Beautiful

You know what God told me about the future? *Nothing*. I have to tell you how troubling this was! But toward the end of my forty days, I realized that God was speaking to me on a very different level. I heard in my spirit that *nothing* is beautiful, as in: Jesus plus *nothing*.

Maybe I was looking for some direction because I was keenly aware of my advancing age (I'm fifty-six) and the fact that this year is the twenty-fifth anniversary of our church. What I wanted to know was specifically what God's will is for the rest of my life. This was answered in a surprising way. This is what I heard, from 1 Thessalonians 5:16–18:

> Be joyful always;
> pray continually;
> give thanks in all circumstances,
> *for this is God's will for you in Christ Jesus* (emphasis mine).

For years, I've taught that God's will is not primarily a place or a particular career. The verses above confirm this, being concerned with character *first* and activity second. I realize this can feel so uncertain, but it's the nature of life and faith. We discover the will of God in the journey, and we don't always know where we are going until after we leave. Paul writes about faith and the future in Philippians:

> Let your gentleness be evident to all. The Lord is near. Do not be anxious about anything, but in everything, by prayer and petition, with thanksgiving, present your requests to God. And the peace of God, which transcends all understanding, will guard your hearts and your minds in Christ Jesus (4:5–7).

The latter part of this passage is fairly familiar to Christians, but the opening verse was a turning point for me during my sabbatical: "Let your gentleness be evident to all. The Lord is near." You see, I don't have a reputation for being a gentle person, but God spoke to my heart:

In every moment of your life, *I am near*. You become anxious when you forget I am near.[4] When you are anxious, you lose your gentleness, because you think you have to make things happen your way. When you are aware that I am near, you know *I am in control*. You are gentle when you know you don't have to make things happen, that I'm right there to take care of your problem and you.

Eugene Peterson in *The Message* translates the rest of this passage as follows:

Don't fret or worry. Instead of worrying, pray. Let petitions and praises shape your worries into prayers, letting God know your concerns. Before you know it, a sense of God's wholeness, everything coming together for good, will come and settle you down. It's wonderful what happens when Christ displaces worry at the center of your life. (Philippians 4:6–7)

Anxiety

Anxiety and depression run together, and sometimes anxiety leads to depressive breakdown. Conversely, depression can be accompanied by free-floating anxiety or agitation. Regardless whether you are suffering from depression or anxiety, or both, and whether or not you know which came first, God's Word has the supernatural power to bring peace in ways we cannot explain logically.

Rich's wife, Sue, found extraordinary comfort and release from her depression when she read, of all books, Lamentations! A dirge about the terrible siege and destruction of Jerusalem in 700 BC, the book was uniquely meaningful to Sue because she could identify with its author, the prophet Jeremiah. She felt a special fellowship with Jeremiah as he wrote about his grief. Ironically, it's in Lamentations, one of the darkest books in the Bible, where we read one of God's most encouraging promises:

My soul is downcast within me.
Yet this I call to mind and therefore I have hope:
Because of the Lord's great love we are not consumed,
     for his compassions never fail.
They are new every morning; great is your faithfulness.
(Lamentations 3:20–23)

His mercies are new *every morning*. Perhaps Jesus had this idea in mind when He said, "Do not worry about tomorrow, for tomorrow will worry about itself. Each day has enough trouble of its own" (Matthew 6:34).

The Sacrament of the Moment

Think for a moment about yesterday. Do you remember yesterday? Where were you? What did you do? How did yesterday influence today? Consider this: *Today was the future yesterday*. Today you are who you are because of what happened in your life and what you did yesterday. *So today—"now"—really matters*. You can't change yesterday, but you can have a huge impact on tomorrow, on the future, by how you live today, right now.

To put this in spiritual terms, when Jesus is Lord of the "right now"—when you acknowledge that "the Lord is near" in every moment of your life—you will conquer the moment. Give the present moment to God and it will transform your future. Listen to what James says about the present and future:

And now I have a word for you who brashly announce, "Today—at the latest, tomorrow—we're off to such and such a city for the year. We're going to start a business and make a lot of money." You don't know the first thing about tomorrow. You're nothing but a wisp of fog, catching a brief bit of sun before disappearing. Instead, make it a habit to say, "If the Master wills it and we're still alive, we'll do this or that." As it is, you are full of your grandiose selves.

All such vaunting self-importance is evil. (James 4:13–16 THE
MESSAGE)

Similarly, Isaiah 40 announces, "He gives strength to the weary
and increases the power of the weak. Even youths grow tired and
weary, and young men stumble and fall; *but those who hope in the
Lord will renew their strength*" (verses 29–31, emphasis mine). I think
I prefer the old King James version on this verse, where it says that
those who "*wait* on the Lord" will become stronger. The Hebrew
term here means to wait *expectantly*. In our frenzied world, waiting
is the last thing we want to do!

The Pause That Refreshes

Waiting is good because it forces us to value the present moment.
When we wait we make every effort to find joy and meet God
there. This is, essentially, the meaning of the Hebrew Sabbath. "Sabbath" and "sabbatical" are from a basic Hebrew term that means
"pause." *Stop*. Stop everything, not just to take a deep breath, but to
think about how God matters in the moment. A Sabbath, a sabbatical, is about letting go of the pressures of your life, your career, your
business, your problems, your future. If you don't, it could kill you:
"For six days, work is to be done, but the seventh day is a Sabbath
of rest, holy to the Lord. Whoever does any work on the Sabbath
day *must be put to death*" (Exodus 31:15, emphasis mine).

Now, we shouldn't take this literally. In fact, Jesus is our Sabbath, and we rest in His finished work. In the broader Christian
community we have tended to downplay the Sabbath, but in our
fear that someone might get legalistic about it, we've neglected the
practical life benefits God offers us when we schedule regular times
of rest. When we don't, we put our health, our families, our careers,
and our souls at risk.

This is the core message of Dan Spaite's book, *Time Bomb in the Church*. It's about burnout and what causes people to collapse emotionally and physically. He's an MD who's made an extraordinary study of the Sabbath and the dreadful consequences of ignoring this God-given cycle of human life—to rest our bodies and souls and to reflect regularly on how God is in control. Many people are emotional car wrecks, deeply depressed, and physically exhausted because, even though they profess to be Christian believers, they've fallen from grace. Some today have used the terms *boundaries* and *margins* to refer to our need for physical, emotional, and spiritual balance, but the idea is as old as the Hebrew Sabbath.

To close, let's look at a powerful passage in Matthew 6:31–34. As you read it prayerfully, let God lift the darkness and give you hope—right now, in this moment.

> So do not worry, saying, "What shall we eat?" or "What shall we drink?" or "What shall we wear?" For the pagans run after all these things, and your heavenly Father knows that you need them. But seek first his kingdom and his righteousness [character first], and all these things will be given to you as well. Therefore do not worry about tomorrow, for tomorrow will worry about itself. Each day has enough trouble of its own.

Don't worry about tomorrow—just take care of the concerns you have today. It's good advice, and I know personally that living like that can make a tremendous difference in de-stressing your life. Perhaps, though, you have some issues in your personality that make this kind of approach to life really hard. Some of us just don't "let go" very easily, as hard as we may try to do so. If you struggle in that area, then the next chapter may have some important insights for you.

chapter 8

Perceptions of Reality:

How Patterns of Thinking Impact Depression

Almost all our misfortunes in life
come from the wrong notions we have about
the things that happen to us.
— Marie Stendhal

Men are not worried by things, but by their
ideas about things. When we meet with
difficulties, become anxious and troubled, let
us not blame others, but rather ourselves;
that is, our ideas about things.
— Epictetus

Thinking straight. It can be a challenge for anyone. And depending upon the makeup of our individual personality, it can be even harder for some of us. In this chapter we want to examine some of the issues of depression that relate to the psychological component of our humanity—and some ways that we can find help by altering our thought patterns.

As in all the other chapters, this is not a one-size-fits-all strategy. The discussion may prove very helpful to you or it may seem less useful than other chapters, since this subject is just one aspect of the puzzling malady called depression. Hopefully, everyone will find some food for thought here and some possible treatments to consider.

I (Gary) wrote this chapter. Rich read it, had some reservations, and sent me an email, which you can read below. These remarks will serve as one of those "precautions" that we talked about in the third chapter—remarks that will alert you to possible "side effects" of what I share in this chapter.

Regarding chapter 8, I really enjoyed it and believe God will use this teaching to help many people. As you read it again, please take a close look at whether someone might erroneously be hearing you say, "Just start thinking straight and your depression will go away." I know you didn't say that, but I had my son read the chapter because he's had depression (yep, it runs in the family), and that was the message that he received. Perhaps it will sort itself out in the context of the entire book.

The medical doctor part of me wants to remind the pastor part of you that some folks with depression are so impaired by their illness that thinking straight is impossible for them. They just don't have the brain "juice" left to make things work right. People with psychotic depression can hallucinate, become badly confused, and develop what we call "psychomotor retardation," that is, they grind to a halt. Psychotherapy for them is pretty useless. They need meds or ECT! Later, if the more radical forms of treatment help, they can sit in on psychotherapy.

The spectrum of this illness runs from these kinds of extreme cases through to the person who is simply stuck in a learned behavioral rut and needs a fresh outlook. One of the D-myths is this: "Stop feeling sorry for yourself and pull yourself up by your bootstraps!" I want to be sure we're sensitive to those folks who have no bootstraps—*or even boots!*

So, with this good caution in mind, let's look at how personality can affect how we react to stresses in life and how changing our thinking can help in both understanding our depression and managing its effects.

Let me (Gary) begin with a confession: Depression isn't my only problem. I have a short fuse too. It's been like this as long as I can remember. My mother could tell you about it. So could my wife, my kids, and the people who have worked with me.

Sometimes I just lose it, especially if I'm tired or under a lot of stress. I've said things I regret terribly, and I've embarrassed myself in public places. I get angry about all the things most people get angry about: other drivers; my lawnmower coughing and sputtering with just two rows of grass left to mow; hanging curtain rods; my dog digging in the garden, uprooting newly planted flowers; differences between my wife and me; and, of course, people at church. I'm probably like you: I get angry when things don't go my way.

Now, I've never physically hurt anybody, and I have never been arrested for getting into a brawl. My anger has never been as bad as it could be, but it's never been as controlled as it should be. And, to make matters worse, my anger at times feeds my depression.

It's commonly known that depression and anger are first cousins. It's been suggested, for example, that depression is anger turned inward. There's truth here, although as we've tried to explain throughout this book, depression is never explained that simply. Certainly, you need to deal with anger and bitterness, but your personality may not change as miraculously as you'd like. Your basic personality is given to you at birth. It is of course somewhat altered by family dynamics, life circumstances, and our perceptions of what has happened to us. But our basic personality profile doesn't usually change radically. All of this is important to keep in mind as we think about depression.

When I became a Christian, God didn't change my personality, because my personality is the way He made me. What does happen, though, is that God takes my imperfect "jar" (2 Corinthians 4:7) and puts it under the lordship of Christ. Take my anger, for example. A positive way for me to look at my anger is to see it as an expression of a deeply passionate personality. I said to a friend's wife one time, "Your husband is a challenge!" She replied quickly, "Yes, he's passionate!"

In the right time and place, under the lordship of Christ, God actually uses my angry side. When I preach, sometimes I sound angry. I can be excitable and exciting too because of my passion. Maybe that's why one of my favorite Scriptures is: "Be ye angry, and sin not" (Ephesians 4:26 KJV). God isn't as obsessed about making my anger go away as I am. If He completely purged me of it, something about my essential nature would change.

Some people probably think I could use a lobotomy. It would really calm me down, and my struggle with my anger would go away forever. But then I would be a terrible preacher. My personality, my gifts—all that makes up "me"—can be used for selfish purposes or as a means of glorifying Christ. When I'm under the lordship of Christ, sanctified and set apart for Him, they all come together as a beautiful thing that blesses others. But when my personality, my gifts, and everything else that makes up "me" are controlled by my selfish nature, I can make my life and the lives of everyone around me thoroughly miserable.

The same thing holds true with people who are prone to depression. Their view of the world is different from the person who does not have it, but it need not prevent them from bringing great benefit to the world. In the last chapter we talked about the apostle Paul. In spite of his driven personality and struggle with some kind of "thorn in the flesh," he managed to pen most of the New Testament and bring the Good News of the gospel to his known world.

I could also mention Martin Luther, Charles Spurgeon, and John

Calvin, all of whom suffered from depression for much of their lives. Of course, we want to take whatever steps we can to overcome depression. Its pain is not something anyone would welcome or discount. I am simply making the point that to suffer from depression does not mean you cannot be a powerfully effective person in the world. Your life can still count for good in a big way.

All of us are affected by how we see the world. For the depressed person, however, it is an even more critical element. As Rich cautioned at the beginning of the chapter, we cannot just "decide" to think differently. It's not that easy, especially when we are under the cloud of depression.

But there is hope for effecting some change if we understand some of the dynamics involved in our thought processes. For the depressed person, *thinking* and *feeling* are hard to distinguish because how you *feel* shades what and how you *think*. Over the years I have discovered that the people and pressures in my life aren't what make me depressed; something inside me makes me depressed. I can be depressed when there isn't a reason in the world to be depressed! Although my darkness deepens in difficult times, mostly my depression is inside me.

Reality is not what happens to me, but what I *think about* happens to me. Recall one of the most painful moments in your past. What was it? Think about it. Talk about it. Chances are, you can't do this without your feelings of anger and resentment bleeding through. It's important to remember which comes first. What you *think* determines how you feel, not the other way around.

Not too long ago I was reading something I had written about the tragic loss of a dear friend's wife. She was thirty-two years old and her untimely and tragic death left him with five children. When I read the story I started to sob. Kathy's death occurred years ago, but when I thought about it all, my emotions begin to resurface.

Not What Happens *to* You

Before we move to the four ways you can change your thoughts for good, allow me to introduce you to a famous psychologist by the name of Albert Ellis, who based his model of therapy on the idea that personal problems are the result of irrational belief systems or patterns of thought. It's called the rational-emotive (thinking-feeling) model of human behavior.

According to Ellis, we experience Activating Events (A) every day that prompt us to look at, interpret, or otherwise *think about* what is occurring. Our interpretation of these events results in specific Beliefs (B) about the event, the world, and our role in the event. Once we develop this belief, we experience Emotional Consequences (C) based solely on our belief, not the event itself.* It looks like this:

$$A \rightarrow B \rightarrow C$$

A is the "Actuating Event," or what happens to you. B is your "Belief," or what you *think* about what happens to you. C is the "Consequence," what you end up doing or feeling as a result of your belief.

Now here's how most of us relate to people and problems. We take no time to think about what we're thinking. We leap from A to C, like this:

$$A \rightarrow C$$

When we skip B—what we *think* about what happened to us—we are prone to blurt out irrationalities like: "*That person* makes me so angry"; "*You* really get to me"; "Her remark embarrassed me terri-

---

*What Gary has presented here comes out of a useful learning theory, but with clinical depression, a primary, fundamental medical problem triggers symptoms and feelings that must be interpreted by the one who suffers from them. The cognitive overlay is this interpretation and includes ideas like "I'm worthless," or "Life's not worth living." The "cognitive overlay" becomes a learned behavior that can sustain the symptoms of depression. (Rich)

bly"; "This weather really is depressing"; "This job bores me"; "The very sight of him makes me want to cry." Without a second thought—and that's the problem!—we leap from A to C. But there's something really important between A and C: *Me!*

$$A \rightarrow B \text{ (me)} \rightarrow C$$

Living by the Truth

The key to life is what each person does at point B—what we believe. We can't control A, the activating event (one example could be depressive symptoms), but if we work on B, we can make C look very different. This overlaps with what we wrote in the preceding chapter, that every moment of your life is an opportunity to turn to God for wisdom and strength. God's input can change B for us. And as a result, our consequences (C) change too.

Albert Ellis, I'm sure, did not frame his ideas based on the Bible. But when we look at the biblical account we can see this pattern for human behavior expressed throughout. For example: "We live by faith, not by sight" (2 Corinthians 5:7). What is Paul telling us here? "Faith" is what we believe and think (B). "Sight" is what we see and hear, what happens to us (A). So ultimate reality for the Christian is what he/she believes, not what he/she sees. Check out these other Bible verses, and see how they substantiate this thinking-feeling model of human behavior:

> Immediately the rooster crowed the second time. *Then Peter remembered* the word Jesus had spoken to him: "Before the rooster crows twice you will disown me three times." And he broke down and wept. (Mark 14:72, emphasis mine)

> By the rivers of Babylon we sat and wept *when we remembered* Zion. (Psalm 137:1, emphasis mine)

I remember my affliction and my wandering, the bitterness and the gall. *I well remember them, and my soul is downcast within me.* Yet *this I call to mind* and therefore I have hope: Because of the Lord's great love we are not consumed, for his compassions never fail. They are new every morning; great is your faithfulness. *I say to myself,* "The Lord is my portion; therefore I will wait for him" (Lamentations 3:19–24, emphasis mine).

Based on the Bible, here's how I modify Ellis' model of human behavior:

The Cross

A → me → C

The Holy Spirit

I am powerless to change the way I think, because my mind is bound by the law of sin and death. I can't change me, no matter how hard I try. The pure power of positive thinking can help a little, but it can't change what's in my heart. I am compelled to bow down to the idols in the chambers of my imagery. Only by dying to self (putting "me" under the cross) and allowing the Holy Spirit to empower me (hold me up) can I change my old pattern of thinking. Only with the help and power of the Holy Spirit will I be able to think the thoughts that will change my life. The apostle Paul knew this well. See what he says in Galatians 5:16–18:

> I say, live by the Spirit, and you will not gratify the desires of the sinful nature. For the sinful nature desires what is contrary to the Spirit, and the Spirit what is contrary to the sinful nature. They are in conflict with each other, so that you do not do what you want [I am powerless]. But if you are led by the Spirit, you are not under law [the futility of human effort].

Four Ways to Change Your Thoughts for Good

1. The big turnaround

Wrong thinking is a result of our sinful nature, and so you may have to begin your process of change by repenting of your wrong beliefs. First, acknowledge and confess to God the dumb things you believe about depression and about yourself, then confess them to someone who can pray for you (1 John 1:8–9 and James 5:16). Repentance, unfortunately, has come to refer to an impractical, even negative religious experience, and generally people have no idea what the word actually means. The New Testament Greek word for *repent* means literally and simply "to change your mind." One very scholarly resource in my personal library defines repentance as "a radical acknowledgment of God . . . as well as a radical confession of sinful fallenness." [1]

Eons ago, before the Great Flood of Noah, the Bible records that "the Lord saw how great man's wickedness on the earth had become, and that *every inclination of the thoughts of his heart* was only evil all the time" (Genesis 6:5, emphasis mine). Centuries later the apostle Paul was still singing the same sad song: "Although they knew God, they neither glorified him as God nor gave thanks to him, but *their thinking became futile and their foolish hearts were darkened*" (Romans 1:21, emphasis mine). Wrong thinking is a sin problem.

2. Bread for the brain

The Bible has the power to change your thoughts for two essential reasons: (1) it's God's Word, and (2) it's the truth. As God's Word, the Bible is much more than a record of things people thought about God. As we mentioned in chapter 6, the Bible has an energy of its own. It's not just a book of good things to think about. It has the power to literally *change your thoughts* when you are powerless.

Paul knew this when he wrote to Timothy that the Scriptures are "God-breathed" (2 Timothy 3:16). This blows right by us today, but for Paul, in his setting, the term *God-breathed* reached back to the opening chapters of the Bible, where it is recorded that God breathed into man the breath of life, and man became a living soul (Genesis 2:7). As human persons are created in the image of God and share in God's life, so the Bible is infused with the life-giving breath and Spirit of God. The power of the Scriptures is the power of the Holy Spirit working in and through God's Word.

Both Hebrew and Greek words for *breath* also mean "spirit." In a clever play on words, Jesus interfaces these ideas of breath, spirit, and life: "The Spirit gives life; the flesh counts for nothing. The words I have spoken to you are spirit and they are life" (John 6:63). The Word of God is, indeed, "living and active. Sharper than any double-edged sword, it penetrates even to dividing soul and spirit, joints and marrow; it judges the thoughts and attitudes of the heart" (Hebrews 4:12). It's powerful! That's why Jesus confronted the very devil himself with Scripture: "It is written," he declared, "Man does not live on bread alone, but on every word that comes from the mouth of God" (Matthew 4:4). If your brain chemistry can be altered by psychotherapy, imagine what the Bible can do for you. The Bible is bread for your brain!

To put the Bible to work for you, especially when you are struggling with deeply entrenched, self-destructive thought patterns, I suggest you become a card-carrying Christian. I'm indebted to best-selling author Norm Wright for this idea. It's simple: take a three-by-five-inch card, and on one side write down the Scripture verse or verses you find especially life-giving for your depression. On the other side, write "STOP!" in large letters.

Carry the card with you. When your thoughts start running away from you, pull out the card and say to yourself (out loud, if possible): "STOP!" Tell your brain, "Stop thinking that way! " Then turn the card over and review the Bible references. Read them again and again, as many times a day as is necessary. This idea is thousands of years old. The psalmist David talked to himself: "Why are you downcast, O my soul? Why so disturbed within me? Put your hope in God, for I will yet praise him, my Savior and my God. My soul is downcast within me; therefore I will remember you" (Psalm 42:5–6).

I'm telling you about this practice because it has helped me big time. I lived on Psalm 20:1–5 for nearly a year. The Bible has a word for this kind of mental exercise—meditation. Meditation is medication for your thought life and your soul: "I remember the days of long ago; I meditate on all your works and consider what your hands have done. I spread out my hands to you; my soul thirsts for you like a parched land. Selah [which means, think about this even more]" (Psalm 143:5–6).

3. Power thoughts through the Holy Spirit

As I mentioned in chapter 6, our minds touch the spiritual realm where both God's spirit and demonic forces are at work. These battles for our minds are real, and we need the resources of heaven to overcome all the wicked devices of our enemy, the devil.

Fortunately, we have what we need to successfully battle in this realm if we know the Lord Jesus. The Holy Spirit lives within us, and He is available to us anytime we call out for His help. When we sense that the thoughts we are having are not from us and conflict with the truth of God's Word, that's the time to do something. Don't just "let it happen" to you—battle back in the power of the Holy Spirit! The apostle Paul wrote, "We do not wage war as the world does . . . We take captive every thought to make it obedient to Christ" (2 Corinthians 10:3, 5). If you need to enlist the prayer support of another Christian, by all means do so.

Depression can involve spiritual warfare, and although this element of the disease may frighten some people, we must address it as a component of a comprehensive approach to understanding and treating depression. As Rich shared with you in chapter 6, his wife, Sue, was helped significantly by recognizing and resisting spiritual darkness.

A year ago, an article about bestselling author Stormie Omartian appeared in *Christianity Today*. Titled "Where Stormie Finds Her Power," author Tim Stafford tells the story of Stormie's extraordinary deliverance from depression. Even after becoming a Christian,

> Omartian continued to struggle with depression. . . . She had daily thoughts of suicide. A church counselor, Mary Anne Pientka, believed that a spirit of oppression was involved. She suggested three days of fasting, followed by a careful regimen of confession and prayer. "When we prayed, that depression lifted," Omartian says. "It was the most amazing thing. I had no idea that could even happen. I felt the depression lift and I thought, 'Okay, this is amazing, this is like taking an aspirin, and you get rid of your headache.' I was assuming it would be back in the morning.
>
> "But the next morning I woke up and it was still gone. And the next, and the next, and the next. I tell you, if I wasn't a believer before, I was then. I was never so shocked. I tell you, it wasn't my faith. It was a demonstration of God's power, and I really had nothing to do with it. I was so amazed. That changed my life."[2]

We're including this story in our book, not to offer a false hope that something similar will happen to everyone with depression who fasts and prays, but to provide a thoroughly biblical view of suffering and depression. We also want to show that a dramatic healing is a genuine possibility. During my recent sabbatical, I (Gary) read through the book of Mark. I was surprised how unfamiliar it felt to me because I've spent so much time in Matthew, Luke, and John. I was deeply moved by how Mark describes the ministry of Jesus mostly in terms of miracles—primarily miracles of demonic deliverance.

We fully realize that if God does something extraordinary for one person, it can be pretty disappointing if He doesn't do the same thing for you. Stafford writes, "Omartian knows that some people need thoughtful counseling as well as prayer. Some people need medical attention. A chemical imbalance requires drug therapy, she says. Omartian also knows that not all prayers get answered as we prefer."[3] But God's stories still must be told, because they raise the level of faith and expectation.

4. Big change may require a painful crisis

Last, but you're going to like this least, the fourth way to change your thoughts is, well, through something you can't make happen, something that is completely out of your control: crisis.

One of the great misbeliefs of the church is the widespread assumption that if you go to Sunday service and someone preaches or teaches God's Word to you, you will change. Yes, God's Word is infused with intrinsic power, and faith comes by hearing the Word of God (see Romans 10:17). But the reality is that *people don't always change because they hear the truth or read good Christian books*. Oh, maybe they do a little, but the changes they make are more like adjustments, like when my car needs a tune-up. It's an altogether different thing when my car needs a new engine because the first engine blew up.

People change radically when the hurricanes of life blow

through their lives. Just *talking about* change changes people only slightly. Really significant change is not a pleasant thing. In fact, it hurts. So in most cases people won't undergo radical change unless the pain to stay the same becomes greater than the pain involved in changing.

My basic personality (Gary) has stayed pretty much the same for the last twenty years, but I sure mellowed out in the late 1980s. In a personal crisis that came out of nowhere, my life was marked forever. It's the dark night of the soul I spoke about in an earlier chapter. Like Jacob, who spent a dark and mysterious night wrestling with an angel and came away from the ford of the Jabbok with a permanently dislocated hip and a new name, Israel, I have been changed by my crisis experience. God didn't change my name, but I still have a mild heart arrhythmia that is similar to Jacob's limp.

Every time I experience a PVC (that's short for preventricular contraction)—and I can feel every single one—I hear the soft voice of God. Sort of like Paul, I can say that I bear on my body the marks of the Lord Jesus (see Galatians 6:17). My heart problem is a *constant reminder* that Jesus is Lord of everything, and I'm lord of nothing. It's that Jesus-plus-nothing, total grace thing again.

I would never want to relive those desperate years again, not for a million bucks. Yet they're a priceless treasure in my life. I could not be who I am today without that crisis or pain. I had to change as a result of it, because the pain to stay the same was killing me.

I wish it were different, but hardship is the way the Lord disciplines us: "'My son, do not make light of the Lord's discipline, and do not lose heart when he rebukes you, because the Lord disciplines those he loves, and he punishes everyone he accepts as a son.' Endure hardship as discipline" (Hebrews 12:5–7). This is why James offers his puzzling invitation to "consider it pure joy . . . whenever you face trials of many kinds" (James 1:2). Doesn't that just make you gnash your teeth? I like the way J. B. Phillips renders this:

> When all kinds of troubles crowd into your lives, my brothers, don't resent them as intruders, but welcome them as friends! Realize that they come to test your faith and to produce in you the quality of endurance. But let the process go on until that endurance is fully developed, and you will find you have become people of mature character, people of integrity with no weak spots.*

I suppose this is the upside of depression. Like Paul, we find ourselves crying to God. If things don't change we must go deeper in our relationship with Him, know that His grace is sufficient for our needs. It's the mature Christian who can welcome adversity as an opportunity to look at himself more deeply and to reach out to God more fervently.

In the next chapter we'll look at some practical helps that are available to us through other people—those who have suffered depression themselves and those who have not. Don't miss out on these opportunities to obtain help. Like all the other strategies we have discussed, they may be an important component to your healing that you've overlooked until now.

---

*J. B. Phillips, *The New Testament in Modern English* (London: G. Bles, 1959).

Other People Can Help:

Communal Strategies for Combating Depression

Just as despair can come to one only from
other human beings, hope, too, can be given
to one only by other human beings.
— ELIE WEISEL

The best cure for worry, depression,
melancholy, brooding, is to go deliberately
forth and try to lift with one's sympathy the
gloom of somebody else.

ARNOLD BENNETT

As a follow-up to chapter 8, let me share some interesting news with
regard to thinking and depression. Recently, the national media
reported some remarkable advances in brain chemistry research. Scientists have discovered that *changing the way you think actually
changes the way the brain functions.* Studies have shown that extended
psychoanalysis and counseling, for example, alter the chemistry of
the brain and, consequently, a person's behaviors. *Psychiatric News*
reported in May 2004:

> For people with mental illness, psychotherapy affects the brain's
> neural networks in much the same way that medicines do, accord-
> ing to Ari Zaretsky, MD, head of the Cognitive Behaviour Therapy

Clinic at Sunnybrook and Women's College Health Sciences Centre and an assistant professor of psychiatry at the University of Toronto. "Many people view psychotropic drugs as the potent interventions, as if they are the biological intervention and psychotherapy is not," said Zaretsky. [However] Zaretsky presented evidence that different forms of psychotherapy can alter the brain's processes for patients with different types of psychiatric disorders in much the same way that antidepressants do.[1]

The American psychologist Thomas Szasz said that "Every act of conscious learning requires the willingness to suffer an injury to one's self-esteem."[2] To find out the most effective means of treating one's depression requires both courage and humility. Why humility? Because we have to be willing to admit the wrong ideas we have held in the past and let them go in order to embrace new information.

The strategies we will look at in this chapter may require the setting aside of some of our prejudices about psychotherapy, counseling, and support groups. Hopefully, we can learn from those who do research with depressed people to see what new breakthroughs are available, and willingly consider how they could be helpful in our overall plan for recovery.

Strong, but Not Independent

Those who live with depression feel weak and vulnerable, but in truth *they are surprisingly strong*. What else but strength of will can explain their ability to bear up under tremendous stress and anxiety every day, and still manage to live their own lives with success and maybe significantly impact the lives of many others? Being *strong* is one thing, but being *independent* is another thing altogether. Those of us who suffer from depression should not see it as a virtue to just stoically forge ahead without ever asking for help along the way.

Allowing other people to help us is both profitable and smart. It does not make us weak to seek out help when it is available.

In chapter 6 we looked at some of the pathways to wholeness that are available in the spiritual realm. Those included prayer and Bible reading, as well as a vibrant relationship with God. Here, we would like to continue that discussion but focus more on the community helps that can also be pathways to wholeness. These involve *other people*, so you must be willing to open yourself up to their input in order to benefit from these. But as the opening paragraph reveals, sometimes these avenues are just as effective in combating depression as medication. Probably using them in combination with medication is the best route of all.

Pathway 1: Friends

Got friends? No one can do life alone. Ironically, though, people who suffer with depression feel so alone, and often they want to be left alone. You can be in a crowd of people at church or at a ball game, but if you're depressed the world around you is surreal. People speak to you. You smile. But you feel nothing. It's like watching a slow-motion video with the sound turned off. The silence in the middle of the carnival of life around you is deafening.

I know. I've felt it—the pain and hopeless despair of loneliness.

I don't need friends to preach at me or give me superficial advice when I'm in the valley of the shadow, but I do need relationships. Back in the late '80s I staggered through the most difficult months of my life. I was *so* depressed. My life was a toxic morass of massive problems in ministry, whipped by the devil himself, it seemed, into my predisposition to be depressed.

Daily I felt a pressure in my chest which, by the end of the year, burst into a serious heart arrhythmia. I was diagnosed with cardiomyopathy at the age of thirty-eight. It was a death sentence, of sorts, because the only cure is a heart transplant. Yet nearly twenty years later, I'm physically fine. God either healed me miraculously or the diagnosis was wrong, which wasn't likely as I had one of the finest, most well-respected cardiologists in the Southwest.

I'm here today to tell the story. When I do—and some elements read like a lurid soap opera—people usually ask, "How did you survive?" Certainly God sustained me. But during that most difficult time in my life, my "dark night of the soul," it was the most important people in my life—my wife and significant friends—who held me together by their love and support. It's not good for men and women to be alone, and we cannot underestimate the power of community. I've written extensively about the necessity of serious relationships in a book called *Leaders that Last*.[3] It is coauthored by a dear friend and counselor, Al Ells, who as much as anyone helped me stay the course.

People in twelve-step programs understand this well: They admit they have a problem, that they are powerless to overcome their problem, and that they need both a higher power and an accountable relationship in order for them to manage and live above their addiction. Here's what the Bible says about this:

> An anxious heart weighs a man down, but a kind word cheers him up. (Proverbs 12:25)

> Let the word of Christ dwell in you richly as you teach and admonish one another with all wisdom, and as you sing psalms, hymns and spiritual songs with gratitude in your hearts to God. (Colossians 3:16)

> But encourage one another daily, as long as it is called Today, so that none of you may be hardened by sin's deceitfulness. (Hebrews 3:13)

Sue Jacobs wouldn't have made it out of the valley of the

shadow without the wisdom, faithfulness, and relentless love of her husband. I know Rich. He's tenacious! We need the support of our spouses, our friends, and the body of Christ—the church. It's important to remember, however, that not everyone will give you good counsel. As we've mentioned throughout this book, some forms of depression need professional care.

Paul wrote this little-known instruction, "Even though you have ten thousand guardians in Christ, you do not have many fathers, for in Christ Jesus I became your father through the gospel" (1 Corinthians 4:15). In other words, every man and woman on the street will freely give you advice about just about anything. Everyone has an opinion, but most don't have informed opinions, and very few people will have your absolute best interests in mind. *So choose your counsel carefully.* Ask yourself: Is this person professionally and/or biblically qualified to help me with my serious condition? Is this person someone who genuinely cares for me?

Which brings us to . . .

Pathway 2: Group therapy and support groups

Judy ached all over. Her fibromyalgia was acting up worse than usual. Her chronic tension headache was like a vise clamped to her skull. Over-the-counter medicines like aspirin and Tylenol were useless against this kind of misery. Judy used the prescription pain-killers her family doctor gave her to make days like these tolerable, but pain-killers did not relieve the inner ache that never left her. The various antidepressant medications that her physician tried only helped a little. Nothing anyone did released Judy from her nagging thoughts of worthlessness and self-recrimination. In fact, these inner voices haunted her more now than ever.

Judy's life had taken a turn for the worse about four months earlier. She and her fiancé, Glen, broke off their wedding engagement after a stormy nine-month romance. Glen was merely the last in a string of abusive relationships. Judy felt all alone. She felt like a failure. She felt like giving up. Instead, she went through the motions of everyday living. She did only what she needed to do. She got up each morning to go to work because she had bills to pay. Other than this, her life revolved around her misery—and her inner thoughts of inadequacy, hopelessness, failure, and gloom.

Judy's depression probably first began late in her teenage years. Her symptoms began after her mom and dad divorced. She suffered aches and pains and chronic headaches, as well as melancholy, hopelessness, and fatigue. As Judy lost interest in school and friends, her grades plummeted, and she became more isolated. She experimented with alcohol and drugs to find relief from her despair. Running away from home and sexual promiscuity made matters more desperate. Judy was a high school dropout with no home, no job, and no hope.

It was at the inner-city homeless shelter that Judy first heard the gospel. She was attracted to the good news of forgiveness and the warmth of Christ's love. She knew this was something she urgently needed. When Judy accepted Jesus as her Savior, her soul flooded with a joy and peace that she had never known or experienced before. Her physical aches and pains and the headaches receded to the background. Although still present, they no longer dominated her life. The shelter provided some vocational training and helped her find a job. In time, Judy earned her GED, got an apartment, and began to take classes at a nearby community college. She also found a church where she joined the singles group. It was here that she met Glen.

At first, Glen seemed like the answer to all of Judy's prayers. He was handsome, smart, charming, and had a good job. A friendship developed into a courtship and later into an engagement. It was after their engagement that Glen began to exhibit controlling and verbally abusive behavior. Judy's old thoughts of failure, inadequacy, and worthlessness began to reappear. A veil of depression descended on her. She broke off her relationship with Glen. Then her life went into another tailspin.

Judy was contacted by the pastor of her singles group when she failed to come to church after several weeks. He referred her to a psychiatrist, who started Judy on psychotherapy. Although Judy's psychiatrist made adjustments in her medication, this did not help her as much as the insights she gained from her counseling sessions. Judy's psychiatrist was able to show her patterns of thinking and cycles of behavior that were hindering her recovery and making her vulnerable to new episodes of depression.

Judy also participated in group therapy sessions where she found other people who understood her and what she was experiencing. Through them she felt less alone and gained insight into her own problems from other members of the group. She also gained the skills to manage her thoughts and emotions more constructively and creatively. Judy was finally on the road to full recovery from chronic depression.

Pathway 3: Professional counseling and psychotherapy

The Bible says, "In abundance of counselors there is victory" (Proverbs 11:14 NASB). So why are Christians so reluctant to get counseling when they need it? Perhaps it is for the same reason that we will not take the medication that has also been shown to help. Judy's story argues against the idea that depression is *only* a biochemical disorder in the brain. She did not respond to a number of anti-depressant medications and did not get well until she underwent psychotherapy and group counseling sessions.

Although scientific evidence shows that people with depression have low brain neurotransmitter levels, depression is much more than "bad brain chemicals." We can't afford to ignore the emotional, spiritual, social, and behavioral dimensions to this illness. This is where pastoral counseling, prayer, psychotherapy, and even group therapy are invaluable to help make a person whole again.

Depression has a profound effect on how people feel, perceive reality, and think about themselves and others. We commonly have negative or distorted thoughts and feelings when we are depressed. In a sense, our depressed brain chemistry colors our ideas and emotions. Traumatic experiences, disappointments, and failures loom larger in our lives when we are depressed. These unpleasant thoughts and feelings become learned behaviors that can perpetuate depression and hinder complete recovery. Fortunately, a skilled psychotherapist or pastor can help a person identify and correct such destructive thinking and behavior. For example, when we are depressed, we tend to personalize or internalize our problems. Our car problems, a broken garbage disposal, and a disappointing phone conversation can become "*my* fault."

Moreover, when we are depressed, we tend to think in absolute or over-generalized terms. When the refrigerator breaks, we think "bad things *always* happen to *me*." Or when an expected bonus is not paid, "good things *never* happen to me." Counseling restores perspective and balance. It trains and equips people in overcoming the distorted thoughts and emotions that arise during the depression so that emotional, mental, and spiritual healing can take place.

Professional counseling also provides important social assistance to those who suffer from depression. Intimacy and social interaction are hard to come by during this illness. Victims of depression lack the energy and confidence to relate to others. Also, people who are depressed are often irritable or anxious, resulting in strained or broken relationships. Counseling can help manage the strain that depression puts on marriages, family relationships, and friendships. It is often helpful to include the spouse or other family members in some of the counseling sessions.

Current medical evidence suggests that counseling and psychotherapy enhance the effectiveness of antidepressant medication. Many therapists believe that psychotherapy is useful in reducing the risk of recurrence of the disease. Also, evidence suggests that if depression recurs in the future, previous psychotherapy may act to reduce its severity. In general, psychotherapy by itself is regarded to be about as effective as antidepressant medication in treating depression. Many physicians believe that psychotherapy's main role is to augment the effectiveness of antidepressant medications.[4] This is an area of continual research and study.

In extreme cases, a patient may be admitted to a hospital under a psychiatrist's care. Special care institutions are the most structured form of community and supportive relationships. The most severely depressed patients need to be hospitalized for their own safety and effective treatment. In general, people with depression are hospitalized when they become confused, suicidal, homicidal, profoundly depressed, or non-functional. The hospital is a controlled environment designed to more closely monitor the patient and to provide intensive therapy, like ECT. (This form of therapy was discussed in some detail in chapter 5.) A hospital setting ensures safety, rest, and immediate help in a time of critical need. Fortunately, only a small proportion of people with depression ever need to be hospitalized.

Pathway 4: Helping others helps you

It's often thought that people who suffer with depression are selfish and only care about themselves. That's a D-myth. People with depression are no more or less selfish than anyone else, yet—and I

(Gary) can speak from my own experience on this—they can be so deeply and inwardly focused that they have difficulty disengaging from their pain and reaching out to others. This can make them *appear* self-absorbed, even selfish. It's like they're living in their own world, which may very well be the case.

In my case, I feel depression most severely in the morning. My wife would tell you I have difficulty getting up, but in fact I have difficulty *waking* up, whether I've slept five hours or nine. Rising early in the morning is torturous for me, and I torture my wife by hitting the Snooze button six or seven times. Even naps leave me feeling dark. When I told my friend Al Ells, a therapist, about this (when I was on a business trip with him), he told me I had the classic symptoms of low-grade chronic depression. He told me his wife had the same difficulty, and medication took the edge off her morning blues, bringing balance into her life. "It will help you too," he said reassuringly.

That's when I began to take therapeutic doses of Serzone. A year or so ago I switched to Celexa. I'm not cured, but the medication helps take the bottom out of my lows, and I especially feel more "normal" in the mornings. Still, not every morning is great, but I find that what often helps me as much as medication is just getting up, getting into the shower, getting going for the day.

Activity, work, meeting with others—becoming intentionally outward-focused, helps my psyche. I realize that busyness is a two-edged sword, that many people plunge into their work and hobbies in an elaborate practice of denial. Simple work, going to work, spending time with others, however, is therapeutic because activity moves me from *inward*-focus to *outward*-focus. This is good. Even better in terms of healing is to become *others*-focused.

Why does helping others help us? Because this is how God made us. He created us in His image, and theologians would agree that the image of God is the interrelational dimension of His triune being. God in himself is a divine community, and as the Bible tells us, God *is* love. Paul writes,

> It's in Christ that we find out who we are and what we are living for. Long before we first heard of Christ and got our hopes up, he had his eye on us, had designs on us for glorious living, part of the overall purpose he is working out in everything and everyone. (Ephesians 1:11–12 THE MESSAGE)

The purpose of God for my life is simple: to bring His love to other people. Jesus explained that the whole of God's word and law can be summarized by two commandments: Love God with everything you have, and love your neighbor as much as you love yourself (see Mark 12:30–31). And *how* do you love your neighbor? Jesus told a story to answer this question: the parable of the Good Samaritan (in Luke 10:30–37). The person who needs you is your neighbor, and you love your neighbor by helping him or her in practical ways. Here's how the apostle John put it:

> This is how we know what love is: Jesus Christ laid down his life for us. And we ought to lay down our lives for our brothers. If anyone has material possessions and sees his brother in need but has no pity on him, how can the love of God be in him? Dear children, let us not love with words or tongue but with actions and in truth. (1 John 3:16–18)

Abraham Lincoln

It's true that not everyone who is severely depressed can get out of bed and help someone else, but many can. It appears that one of our greatest presidents, Abraham Lincoln, was stricken with depression. In an extraordinary article on "Lincoln's Great Depression" in *Atlantic,* Joshua Wolf Shenk writes,

Lincoln connected his mental well-being to divine forces. As a young man he saw how religion could ameliorate life's blows, even as he found the consolation of faith elusive . . . Lincoln charted his own theological course to a living vision of how frail, imperfect mortals could turn their suffering selves into the service of something greater and find solace—not in any personal satisfaction or glory *but in dutiful mission*.[5](emphasis mine)

Lincoln brought a sense of purpose and peace to his troubled soul by pouring his life into saving the nation. *Helping others helps you,* because helping others turns you inside out and draws you closer to God. Helping others is an important pathway to wholeness: "Give, and it will be given to you. A good measure, pressed down, shaken together and running over, will be poured into your lap. For with the measure you use, it will be measured to you" (Luke 6:38). Read on as Darrel Mullins tells his story of pain, discouragement, and depression—and how he found healing for himself by helping others.

A young man in a monster SUV slammed into the back of my small car. Of the four passengers, no one seemed seriously hurt. I felt pain, but I thought I could press through it. When the pain in my shoulder grew worse, I scheduled an MRI, and my doctor diagnosed my problem: mild tendinitis.

Mild tendinitis? My shoulder was killing me! So I made an appointment with a well-respected orthopedic surgeon. Without even reviewing the MRI, he told me I had a tear of the labium that could only have been detected *immediately after* the accident in an MRI with the presence of blood. Next stop: shoulder surgery.

In the eighth week of post-op therapy, while lying on the floor watching TV, I got up using my good arm and directly on my right elbow—POP. The pain was indescribable and I knew immediately I had damaged my shoulder *again*. Where was God's plan for my new beginning? Doubt, fear, anxiety came—and my first real taste of feelings of depression entered my soul. Outdoor activities, functions with family and friends, travel, and intimate relationship all came to a screeching halt.

After a second surgery, while being stretched during therapy, we all heard another *pop* and I felt searing pain! *Not again!* Back to the surgeon. Another MRI showed massive scar tissue and lesions in my shoulder—a monumental setback. One night, having difficulty sleeping, I crawled—shaking and crying—into a corner of our house. Me, the man. It terrified my wife, Teela.

Our church, Word of Grace, where Gary is our senior pastor, agreed to answer our city's appeal for help for the homeless during the hot and deadly Phoenix summer of 2005. News of heat-related deaths made national news. Teela and I committed to assist with our new day center for the homeless *every day* for nearly two months.

We believed that helping others with extraordinary needs would ease the anger and pain I held inside because of my unfortunate situation. And we were right. In just a couple of days my focus was where it was supposed to be: not on me. Our "Beat the Heat" ministry wasn't just for scores of homeless guests; as I daily served those desperate people in wretched circumstances, I began to climb out of my Grand Canyon of despair.

I needed to help others to help myself. Helping the poor—seeing the appreciation in their eyes for our love and care—was God's prescription for my feelings of depression. My pain isn't gone, and my shoulder isn't healed. And if I'm not careful, I fall back into the darkness of self-pity and despair. But helping others is the *only* relief I've had in my personal darkness.

Amazing, isn't it? Something as simple as helping less fortunate people can radically change how we feel about ourselves and life in general. As we have said over and over again in this book, this may not be the answer for you. But we share it in case it does provide that one key ingredient that lifts you from the pit of depression.

People need people. It's not good for people to take on life alone. So don't let your pride, your prejudices, your cynicism, or your fears keep you from finding real help in your battle with depression. You'll never know how these avenues will impact you until you give them a try. Our hope is that these communal pathways to healing, used in combination with the right medications, a growing relationship with God, and new ways of looking at life, will round out your strategies for combating and overcoming depression.

However, we would be dishonest if we promised that if you do all these right things, sooner or later you will find complete relief from your depression. For those of you who, despite your best efforts to overcome depression, continue to suffer from its effects, we want to offer comfort and encouragement in your journey. The final chapter is for you.

chapter 10

When Depression Just Won't Go Away:

Living Above Your Pain

*I've tried everything and nothing helps. I'm at the end
of my rope. Is there no one who can do anything for
me? Isn't that the real question?*
—ROMANS 7:24 THE MESSAGE

In follow-up research it has been found that some people (about 20
percent) can eventually stop taking depression medication, but most
(the remaining 80 percent) need to take their medication indefinitely.
For example, if someone has two or more major clinical depressive
episodes, then lifelong maintenance of antidepressant medication is
usually required.

We would like to think that for everyone, sooner or later, medication would not be necessary. When that doesn't happen it troubles
us deeply, because it raises huge questions about God, personal
change, and the potentials of human life. In this final chapter we
want to look at how we can respond when, despite all our best
efforts at recovery, our depression will not leave. While we should
always hope and work toward full recovery, and pray to that end,

we are sometimes left with the reality of an ongoing problem with depression.

There are many things we *can do* to deal with depression in ourselves and others. We've looked at some of them in this book. Yet we live in an imperfect, fallen world. Human life has limitations, and sometimes those limitations are painfully severe. Life isn't always what we know it should be; we stand and watch hopelessly as some things never seem to change. We wonder too why an omnipotent God doesn't put an end to sin and suffering—right now. He could. He should. But He doesn't.

As I (Gary) mentioned in chapter 8, I struggle with an anger problem in addition to occasional bouts with depression. As a pastor, you can imagine how embarrassing this can be at times. You can be assured that I've prayed about my anger and depression. I've fasted for freedom, received professional counsel and prayer, read books about it, even preached on it.

And now Rich and I are writing a book about depression—but not to tell you how to overcome it in five easy steps. That's just not possible. We know that many people have experienced the miracle-working power of God and, consequently, have been immediately and permanently healed from depression. We rejoice that God can do anything and everything! But most of life isn't like that. It's blandly routine, and change in our lives is usually a slow and difficult process. (Sometimes painfully slow.) Worst of all, sometimes *nothing changes*. And this reality flies in the face of a particularly powerful myth that most of us believe:

If I pray enough and work on it, someday my problem will go away completely.

Want a simple reason why I know this is a myth? We're not in heaven yet! Heaven is the place where everything is made right— where there will be no more pain, tears, and sorrow. No injustice or depression. But until we get there, our bodies continue to age and people still struggle, just as Paul did, with things beyond their ability to control.[1]

Leaving the Shadowlands

I come to Christ "just as I am," but I can't stay that way; every Bible verse, every sermon, every song, reminds me that I should be different. Instead of lingering in the dark shadow of who I am, I long to live in the blinding light of what I *should be*. So why do I get stuck? I'm so glad that the apostle Paul wrestled with this same problem:

> I find this law at work: When I want to do good, evil is right there with me. For in my inner being I delight in God's law; but I see another law at work in the members of my body, waging war against the law of my mind and making me a prisoner of the law of sin at work within my members. What a wretched man I am! Who will rescue me from this body of death? (Romans 7:21–24)

The church is an environment where we expect, even insist on, radical change. Often it is viewed as a necessary condition for acceptance, seeing people's lives change for the better. If they don't, we suspect that God may not be in them after all. Physician and Christian counselor Dwight Carlson calls this the myth of the emotional health gospel, which "assumes that if you have repented of your sins, prayed correctly, and spent adequate time in God's Word, you will have a sound mind."[2]

On the one hand, we must agree that change should come— followers of Jesus should become more and more like Jesus. So the church must continue to be relentless in its pursuit of Christlikeness. That's the core of discipleship. But the rub comes when we don't allow change to come in God's time and through His chosen means of accomplishing it. And before we see the dramatic changes we expect to occur, we must understand that there will be lots of opportunities to extend forgiveness to those who aren't there yet. We must be just as relentless in accepting people who are struggling to change but are finding the process longer and harder than anyone expected. Profound change is not an automatic result of being a Christian. It occurs only when God steps into our utterly debilitating weaknesses and shows His strength, something we call *grace*. I believe this is what Paul meant when he confessed,

> At first I didn't think of it as a gift, and begged God to remove it [the thorn]. Three times I did that, and then he told me,
>
> My grace is enough; it's all you need.
> My strength comes into its own in your weakness.
>
> Once I heard that, I was glad to let it happen. I quit focusing on the handicap [keep this term in mind as you read on] and began appreciating the gift. It was a case of Christ's strength moving in on my weakness. Now I take limitations in stride, and with good cheer, these limitations that cut me down to size—abuse, accidents, opposition, bad breaks. I just let Christ take over! And so the weaker I get, the stronger I become. (2 Corinthians 12:8–10 THE MESSAGE)

As we explained in an earlier chapter, Paul's thorn—the thing that just wouldn't go away—was very possibly depression. *But finding grace to live with it gave him the power to live above it.*

Emotional Disabilities

In the world today it's still okay to use the word *handicap* when you're talking about your bad golf game, but people who have physical limitations are not so likely to use it. I take that on the word of a dear friend, David, a paraplegic who informed me that handicap has its roots in the "handy cap" that "crippled" people held out to collect change from people passing by.

Disabled and *physically challenged* are much less demeaning terms. Shamefully, I confess I was clueless about the issues of accessibility until I experienced David's subculture firsthand. I watched his extraordinary effort in so many settings—waiting for him to get in and out of his specially designed van, pushing his wheelchair through a crowded basketball arena concourse, standing in line for fast food, getting in and out of restaurants, sitting in the "accessible seating" deep in the end zone of an NFL game. I heard it also as I listened carefully to David's concerns when we designed our new worship center.

Men and women who are physically challenged can't just *will themselves* into health. We recognize that they have to learn how to accept their disability and make the best of life in spite of it. We sort of understand. At least we try. At least we don't ask people in wheelchairs to play tackle football.

But what about people with emotional problems? Are they *disabled*? Are they emotionally challenged? Or can they, should they, just shake themselves out of their depression, their gloom, and their personal sadness?

"The prejudice against those with emotional problems," Dwight Carlson writes, "can be seen in churches across the nation on any Sunday morning. We pray publicly for the parishioner with cancer or a heart problem or pneumonia. But rarely will we pray publicly for Mary with severe depression, or Charles with incapacitating panic attacks, or the minister's son with schizophrenia. Our silence subtly conveys that these are not acceptable illnesses for Christians to have."[3]

Right this minute I'm not depressed, but melancholy can come on me as suddenly as a summer thunderstorm in Oklahoma. Sometimes I can feel the depression in my head, literally, like when you feel the effects of drinking a glass of wine or the caffeine rush in a huge cup of Starbucks coffee. When I feel depressed, I can't just shake it off or make it go away. So I do the next best thing: I accept myself and offer no apologies for who I am.

No Excuses

My friend in the wheelchair, David, never complained. He wasn't bitter, or if he was, he never gave me a clue. A graduate of the University of Arizona, he was a millionaire partner in a hugely successful microchip business here in Phoenix. David was and continues to be an extraordinary inspiration to me because he made no excuses. He steadfastly refused to let his disability get the best of him. Knowing that it wouldn't just go away, he did everything he could to live *with* it and live *above* it. That's how I feel about my emotional disabilities. I can't make them go away, but I'm not going to let them get the best of me either.

Like the apostle Paul.

Jesus models righteousness, and I follow Him, but Paul models how a man with explosive passions follows Jesus. "Follow my example," Paul wrote, "as I follow the example of Christ" (1 Corinthians 11:1). Let's look, then, at what Paul says about his effort to become more like Christ:

> I do not understand what I do. For what I want to do I do not do, but what I hate I do. And if I do what I do not want to do, I agree that the law is good. As it is, it is no longer I myself who do it, but it is sin living in me. I know that nothing good lives in me, that is, in my sinful nature. For I have the desire to do what is good, but I cannot carry it out. (Romans 7:15–18)

This is one of the most difficult aspects of being a Christian. It's a uniquely Christian predicament, because believers are painfully aware of the gaping gulf between who they are and what God says they should be. Like Paul, we desperately want to live for God but find that something inside keeps holding us back. After a while, sometimes after *years* of trying to overcome some weakness, we can feel an overwhelming sense of condemnation:

> So I find this law at work: When I want to do good, evil is right there with me. For in my inner being I delight in God's law; but I see another law at work in the members of my body, waging war against the law of my mind and making me a prisoner of the law of sin at work within my members. *What a wretched man I am! Who will rescue me from this body of death?* (Romans 7:21–24, emphasis mine)

Living With Who You Are, Because God Does

Isn't that every person's desperate appeal from time to time? It's mine, and when I read these verses in Romans 7, I'm saying to myself, *Yes! Yes! Paul is going to tell me how to heal my troubled soul.* His answer comes in verse 25: "Thanks be to God through Jesus Christ our Lord!"

Yes! Yes!

But wait . . . Thanks be to God *for what?*

Does Paul promise here that Jesus is going to work a miracle and change me forever? *No.* So just what are you saying, Paul? Look at the verse again: "Thanks be to God—through Jesus Christ our Lord!" Paul is giving thanks to God through Jesus, but he doesn't say specifically, "Thanks be to God *because* Jesus delivers me." It seems like that would be the perfect conclusion. Instead, Paul ends the seventh chapter of Romans by boomeranging back to the problem and leaving us in the lurch: "So then, I myself in my mind am a slave to God's law, but in the sinful nature a slave to the law of sin."

That's it? That's just the way it is? Is there no way out? The end of Romans 7 seems so unresolved that Eugene Peterson's *The Message* puts words in Paul's mouth: "The answer, thank God, is that Jesus Christ can and does." I love Eugene Peterson's work . . . but how can he do that? I'll tell you how: We Christians just can't bring ourselves to accept the fact of the war raging in our souls, especially the fact that it *will not end in this life.*

I believe that's why Paul (the realist) ends Romans 7 with this statement of reality: "So then, I myself in my mind am a slave to God's law, but in the sinful nature a slave to the law of sin" (v. 25). Someone in a Christian twelve-step program might say it like this: "In my heart I'm a child of God, but in my sinful nature I always have been and always will be an alcoholic." Are we sentenced, then, to live in the captivity of our weaknesses forever? A thousand times, NO!

Pay attention now: My hope is not that someday, when I am spiritual enough, I will "arrive," and for the rest of this life I'll never have a problem with anger or depression or whatever. Instead, there is a verse that—like a cosmic cathedral bell—rings out a deafening declaration of assurance and hope: *"There is now no condemnation for those who are in Christ Jesus"* (Romans 8:1).

In an interview on-line, Caly (her last name is withheld) was asked to describe her biggest triumph since her diagnosis of depression. It doesn't indicate that she is a follower of Christ, but her answer sounds like Romans 8:1. "This may sound silly to anyone who has not experienced depression, but it was a triumphant day when I could finally look in the mirror and say, 'Caly, *you* are a *good* person' . . . and truly believed it. This has made all the difference in my life." [4]

If only every *Christian* could feel that way about themselves! As a believer, I'm not just a *good* person; according to Hebrews 10:14, the once and final sacrifice of Christ has made me *perfect forever*! That's why *now* there's *no* condemnation for me, even though at times it seems I have plenty wrong with me, plenty to justify condemning myself.

Saved by Faith, Living by Faith

I'm saved by faith in the finished work of Christ. Most Christians have that one down pat. But I have to keep reminding myself that I'm *living* by faith in the finished work of Christ too. Paul, quoting the Old Testament prophet Haggai, announced, "The righteous will live by faith" (Galatians 3:11).

In his wonderful book *The Wisdom of Accepted Tenderness,* Brennan Manning writes,

> The crux of this little book can be stated briefly ... In a moment of naked honesty, ask yourself, "Do I wholeheartedly trust that God likes me?" (Not *loves* me, because theologically God can't do otherwise.) "And do I trust that God likes me, not after I clean up my act and eliminate every trace of sin, selfishness, dishonesty, and degraded love; not after I develop a disciplined prayer life and spend ten years in Calcutta with Mother Teresa's missionaries; but in this moment, right now, right here, with all my faults and weaknesses?" If you answer without hesitation, "Oh yes, God does like me; in fact, he's very fond of me," you're living in the wisdom of accepted tenderness.[5]

The righteousness of Christ is free—from start to finish. That's why Paul could write at the very end of Romans 8:

> So, what do you think? With God on our side like this, how can we lose? If God didn't hesitate to put everything on the line for us, embracing our condition and exposing himself to the worst by sending his own Son, is there anything else he wouldn't gladly and freely do for us? And who would dare tangle with God by messing

with one of God's chosen? Who would dare even to point a finger? The One who died for us!—who was raised to life for us!—is in the presence of God at this very moment sticking up for us.

Do you think anyone is going to be able to drive a wedge between us and Christ's love for us? There is no way! Not trouble, not hard times, not hatred, not hunger, not homelessness, not bullying threats, not backstabbing, not even the worst sins listed in Scripture. . . . None of this fazes us because Jesus loves us. I'm absolutely convinced that nothing—nothing living or dead, angelic or demonic, today or tomorrow, high or low, thinkable or unthinkable—absolutely nothing can get between us and God's love because of the way that Jesus our Master has embraced us. (vv. 8:31–35, 37–39 THE MESSAGE)

Finishing the Race Is What Counts

I'm determined to live by faith in God's relentless, measureless, incomprehensible, unconditional love for me, and I'm not going to hang my life on the hope that someday I'll never have any more problems. That day is called heaven, and until I get to heaven, I'm not going to trust in my wobbly, wavering goodness. *Really depressed—mildly depressed—not depressed at all* is not a barometer of my relationship with God! My hope is in Christ, in His perfect work on the cross to forgive me perfectly. I *am* perfect in Christ, right now, because of His grace: "I no longer live, but Christ lives in me. The life I live in the body, I live by faith in the Son of God, who loved me and gave himself for me" (Galatians 2:20).

This fills me with such hope that my melancholy is, well, gone—at least for now. In other words, healing comes into my life when I accept myself for who I am because God accepts me fully in spite of who I am. A reality of life is that some problems will cling to your life like super glue. When they don't go away, what are you going to do? *You must learn to become content, no matter what the circumstances.* Medication and radical treatment for your depression may get you back on the road of recovery, but you may never be entirely like other people who have never had a bout with major depression.

I suppose it's like running a race. One person will always cross the finish line first. Everyone else is an also-ran, but everyone else can also finish the race!

> Do you see what this means—all these pioneers who blazed the way, all these veterans cheering us on? It means we'd better get on with it. Strip down, start running—and never quit! No extra spiritual fat, no parasitic sins. *Keep your eyes on Jesus, who both began and finished this race we're in. Study how he did it. Because he never lost sight of where he was headed—that exhilarating finish in and with God—he could put up with anything along the way: cross, shame, whatever.* And now he's there, in the place of honor, right alongside God. When you find yourselves flagging in your faith, go over that story again, item by item, that long litany of hostility he plowed through. That will shoot adrenaline into your souls! (Hebrews 12:1–3 THE MESSAGE, emphasis mine)

Holy and Merciful God: You know me, inside and out. You know what I'm struggling with inside, and you accept me fully, knowing that I will never be perfect in this lifetime. There is now no condemnation in your heart for me. You accept me, so I will accept myself. Amen.

Twenty-five Common Myths About Depression
. . . and where we discuss them in the book

1. Depression is a mental illness. People with depression are "crazy." It's all in their heads. (Chapters 1, 2, 3, 5, 8, 10)
2. Depression is a character flaw. If you can't snap out of your depression, it means you're weak. Depression is from inadequate coping skills or laziness. (Chapters 1, 2, 3, 5, 9, 10)
3. Depression is completely of the person's own making. It's their fault they're depressed. (Chapters 1, 2, 3, 5, 9, 10)
4. Depression is sadness. People with depression just need to cheer up and count their blessings. They need to stop feeling sorry for themselves. (Chapters 1, 3, 6, 8, 10)
5. Depression is a means of getting attention. People with depression are immature. (Chapters 1, 2, 3, 4, 9, 10)
6. Depression is only a physical illness. All people with depression simply have a genetic biochemical abnormality. (Chapters 3, 4, 6, 9, 10)
7. Depression occurs because we lack a strong relationship with God. Christians should not get depressed. (Chapters 1, 2, 4, 6, 9, 10)
8. Antidepressant medications are "happy pills." They are "uppers" or mood elevating drugs. (Chapters 1, 2, 5)
9. Antidepressants are addicting or habit forming. You can become dependent on them. (Chapters 1, 5)
10. Antidepressants change your personality. They make you into someone else. (Chapters 1, 2, 5, 8)

11. Taking an antidepressant means you lack faith. You should always only seek a "faith healing." (Chapters 1, 2, 3, 5, 6)
12. Antidepressant medication is a cure for depression. Once your depression goes away, it won't come back again. (Chapters 1, 2, 4, 5, 6, 9, 10)
13. There's nothing you can do to prevent your depression from coming back again. (Chapters 1, 2, 3, 4, 5, 7, 8, 9, 10)
14. Counseling and psychotherapy are unnecessary, especially if you take medication. (Chapters 3, 4, 9)
15. There's nothing you can do if you're depressed. You must rely on the interventions of health care providers only. You are helpless. (Chapters 1, 2, 4, 5, 6, 7, 8, 9, 10)
16. If someone is depressed, there must be some external thing bothering them, like divorce, financial crisis, or a death in the family. (Chapters 1, 2, 3, 4, 8, 10)
17. Depressed people with suicidal ideas are just seeking attention; they won't commit suicide. (Chapters 1, 3, 4, 5, 6)
18. Depression is something of which to be ashamed. (Chapters 1, 2, 3, 6, 7, 10)
19. Depression is only a problem in developed, industrialized nations. People in developing countries with simpler lifestyles do not get depression. (Chapters 3, 7)
20. Electroconvulsive Therapy (ECT, or "shock treatment") is a barbaric, painful treatment that should never be employed today. (Chapters 5, 9)
21. Children do not get depressed. It is an illness of adults. (Chapters 3, 4)
22. If you can wait it out, depression will eventually just go away. (Chapters 1, 2, 3, 4, 6, 9, 10)
23. Depression is the natural outcome of poor nutritional habits, lack of exercise, or unhealthy lifestyle. (Chapters 2, 4, 5)
24. Depression can be cured by positive thinking and denial. (Chapters 6, 8, 9, 10)
25. Depressed people are non-functional. If they go to work and look "normal," they're not depressed. (Chapters 1, 2, 4, 7, 9, 10)

appendix **B**

The History and Development of Antidepressant Medications

Antidepressant medications were discovered by accident in the early 1950s. The first modern antidepressant, iproniazid (i-pro-*nye*-ah-zid), was an antibiotic developed by researchers to treat tuberculosis ("TB" or "consumption"). It came as a surprise to doctors to discover that depressed TB patients treated with this drug recovered from their depression but not from their TB. By 1957, scientists had published several studies showing the effectiveness of iproniazid on depression.*

One year later, over four hundred thousand patients with depression were taking this antibiotic—not for TB, but for clinical depression! Investigators later discovered that iproniazid helped depression by hampering the enzyme in the brain that destroys certain key neurotransmitters, called "monoamines" (like dopamine, norepinephrine, and serotonin). For this reason, the new class of drugs was called **M**onoamine **O**xidase **I**nhibitors (MAOIs). The chemical action of MAOIs restores brain monoamine neurotransmitters to normal levels, which alleviates the symptoms of depression.

Iproniazid is no longer used to treat depression. It had too many side effects and was too toxic for general use. But its discovery helped doctors understand what causes depression in many patients. It also gave physicians insight into how depression could be treated.

Today, MAOIs include drugs like isocarboxazid (trade name: Marplan), tranylcypromine (trade name: Parmate), and phenelzine

---

*C. B. Nemeroff, "Advancing the Treatment of Mood and Anxiety Disorders: The first 10 years' experience with paroxetine," *Psychopharmacol Bull* (Suppl 1) 37 (2003): 6–7.

(trade name: Nardil). MAOIs are not used as much today because of their side effects. These include dizziness, weakness, headaches, and trembling. Also, MAOIs can have dangerous interactions with certain foods and medications. Even over-the-counter flu and cold remedies can interact with MAOIs to cause life-threatening reactions. For this reason, scientists searched for other types of antidepressant agents that might have a similar mechanism of acting.

Interestingly enough, the second major class of antidepressant medication was also discovered by accident at about the same time as MAOIs.† Physicians were searching for a treatment for schizophrenia. A drug called imipramine was tried on these patients in the mid-1950s. Although imipramine did not help the schizophrenia sufferers, doctors noticed marked improvement in depressed patients. This led to the discovery of the tricyclic class of antidepressants (named after the chemical structure of these agents). In time, doctors found that tricyclic antidepressants, like imipramine, also increased the activity of monoamine neurotransmitters by preventing their absorption ("reuptake") back into the nerves. This allowed the neurotransmitter levels to remain at normal levels.

The tricyclic antidepressants are easier and safer to use than MAOIs. They are better tolerated by patients. Common side effects for tricyclic drugs include a dry mouth, constipation, blurred vision, difficulty urinating, worsening glaucoma, and fatigue. Tricyclics should be used with caution in elderly patients, who are more vulnerable to their side effects. These medications can affect heart rate, rhythm, and blood pressure. An overdose with tricyclic antidepressants can cause fatal heart symptoms. Included in the tricyclic drug class are medications like amitriptyline (trade name: Elavil), desipramine (trade name: Norpramin), imipramine (trade name: Tofranil),

---

†T. A. Ban, "Pharmacotherapy of Depression: A historical analysis," *J Neural Transm* 108, no. 6 (2001): 707–16.

and nortriptyline (trade names: Aventyl, Pamelor). Because of the side effects of tricyclic antidepressants, and because of the dangers of overdosing on them, scientists searched for safer medications that were equally effective. It was hoped that a medicine that was selective in its beneficial effects on neurotransmitters would avoid many adverse side effects of treatment. This led to the development of a new class of agents called the Selective Serotonin Reuptake Inhibitors, or SSRIs.

The discovery of the SSRIs was a breakthrough in the treatment of depression. They have few side effects and are safer than older antidepressant drugs. They are *not* more effective than older agents, however. Some patients who do not respond well to SSRIs do respond very well to older medications, like the MAOIs or tricyclic antidepressants. Because SSRIs have few side effects, they are well-suited for long-term, maintenance therapy. When side effects are experienced with SSRIs, they include difficulty with sexual arousal, headache, insomnia, reduced appetite or nausea, and a dry mouth.

Most symptoms resolve with time. If SSRIs are stopped abruptly, patients experience agitation, nervous changes, tremor, diarrhea, fever, and other problems. For this reason, SSRIs should be tapered slowly before they are discontinued. SSRI medications include citalopram (trade name: Celexa), escitalopram (trade name: Lexapro), fluoxetine (trade name: Prozac), paroxetine (trade names: Paxil, Pexeva), and sertraline (trade name: Zoloft).

There are now many classes of antidepressant medications. Medical research adds new drugs each year. One new class of antidepressant selectively targets both serotonin *and* norepinephrine. Serotonin and Norepinephrine Reuptake Inhibitors (SNRIs) include venlafaxine (trade name: Effexor) and duloxetine (trade name: Cymbalta). Side effects include constipation, loss of appetite, sexual problems, increased heart rate, and cholesterol levels. A similar selective drug effect strategy is employed by the Norepinephrine and Dopamine Reuptake Inhibitors (NDRIs). Bupropion (trade name: Wellbutrin) is an example of this type of drug. Bupropion can cause seizures in vulnerable people. Insomnia, agitation, and intense dreaming are also described. Other drugs that use combined receptor action include trazodone (trade name: Desyrel), nefazodone (trade name: Serzone), and mirtazapin (trade name: Remeron). Side effects include dry mouth, nausea, and dizziness.

This brief summary does not begin to explore everything about antidepressant medications. It takes considerable knowledge, skill, and experience to use these drugs safely and effectively. For this reason, antidepressants should be prescribed and managed by qualified physicians only.

Are You Depressed?

A useful depression screening self-test was published in medical literature in 1965.* Called the "Zung Self-Rating Depression Scale," this test has been adapted several times since then. The test has twenty questions. To take the test, place a mark (check or X) in the column that best answers each question. When answering the questions, think about how you've felt *over the last two weeks*.

Each question, and its response, is weighed differently (between 1 and 4). To score your self-test, consult the key that is included in this appendix. Total up the score from your answers to the questions. The highest possible score is 80. If you scored 50 or higher, you may be depressed and should consult your physician for further evaluation. This test is not perfect, but it is a useful tool to screen for depression.

---

*W. Zung, "A Self-Rating Depression Scale," *Arch Gen Psychiatry*, 12 (1965): 63–70.

Take the Zung Self-Rating Depression Test

Put a check mark in the appropriate column.

	Seldom	Some-times	Often	Usually
1. I feel downhearted and blue.				
2. Morning is when I feel the best.				
3. I have crying spells or feel like it.				
4. I have trouble sleeping at night.				
5. I eat as much as I used to.				
6. I still enjoy sex.				
7. I notice that I am losing weight.				
8. I have trouble with constipation.				
9. My heart beats faster than usual.				
10. I get tired for no reason.				
11. My mind is as clear as it used to be.				
12. I find it easy to do the things I used to.				
13. I am restless and can't keep still.				
14. I feel hopeful about the future.				
15. I am more irritable than usual.				
16. I find it easy to make decisions.				
17. I feel that I am useful and needed.				
18. My life is pretty full.				
19. I feel others would be better off if I were dead.				
20. I still enjoy the things I used to do.				

Score the Zung Self-Rating Depression Test

Add up your score based on the key below.

	Seldom	Some-times	Often	Usually
1. I feel downhearted and blue.	1	2	3	4
2. Morning is when I feel the best.	4	3	2	1
3. I have crying spells or feel like it.	1	2	3	4
4. I have trouble sleeping at night.	1	2	3	4
5. I eat as much as I used to.	4	3	2	1
6. I still enjoy sex.	4	3	2	1
7. I notice that I am losing weight.	1	2	3	4
8. I have trouble with constipation.	1	2	3	4
9. My heart beats faster than usual.	1	2	3	4
10. I get tired for no reason.	1	2	3	4
11. My mind is as clear as it used to be.	4	3	2	1
12. I find it easy to do the things I used to.	4	3	2	1
13. I am restless and can't keep still.	1	2	3	4
14. I feel hopeful about the future.	4	3	2	1
15. I am more irritable than usual.	1	2	3	4
16. I find it easy to make decisions.	4	3	2	1
17. I feel that I am useful and needed.	4	3	2	1
18. My life is pretty full.	4	3	2	1
19. I feel others would be better off if I were dead.	1	2	3	4
20. I still enjoy the things I used to do.	4	3	2	1

As already mentioned, if you scored 50 or higher you may be depressed. You should consult your physician for further evaluation.

Resources*

Books:

David B. Biebel, DMin and Harold G. Koening, MD. *New Light on Depression: Help, Hope, and Answers for the Depressed and Those Who Love Them*. Grand Rapids, MI: Zondervan, 2004. Christian perspective.

Don Colbert, MD. *The Bible Cure for Depression and Anxiety*. Lake Mary, FL: Siloam, A Strang Company, 1999. This simple and helpful book has sold more than 2.5 million copies.

Elyse Fitzpatrick and Laura Hendrickson, MD. *Will Medicine Stop the Pain? Finding God's Healing for Depression, Anxiety and Other Troubling Emotions*. Chicago: Moody Publishers, 2006. Christian approach.

Bonnie Keen. *A Ladder Out of Depression: God's Healing Grace for the Emotionally Overwhelmed*. Eugene, OR: Harvest House, 2005. Written mostly for women; Christian perspective.

Paul Meier, MD. *Blue Genes: Breaking Free From the Chemical Imbalances That Affect Your Moods, Your Mind, Your Life, and Your Loved Ones*. Carol Stream, IL: Tyndale House Publishers, 2006. A Focus on the Family book produced in cooperation with Tyndale.

Anne Sheffield. *How You Can Survive When They're Depressed: Living and Coping With Depression Fallout*. New York: Three Rivers Press/Crown Publishing Group, 1999. For those living with depressed people; secular perspective.

Web Sites

National Institute of Mental Health—Depression: Does This Sound
Like You?
http://www.nimh.nih.gov/publicat/nimhstoriesdepression.cfm
University of Michigan—Beyond Sadness, a multilanguage information resource on depression
http://www.med.umich.edu/depression/brochures.htm
National Institute of Mental Health—General information about
bipolar disease
http://www.nimh.nih.gov/healthinformation/bipolarmenu.cfm
American Academy of Child and Adolescent Psychology—Warning
signs for teen suicide
http://www.aacap.org/publications/factsfam/suicide.htm
National Institute of Mental Health—General information about
antidepressant medications
http://www.nimh.nih.gov/publicat/medicate.cfm#ptdep7
http://cms.psychologytoday.com/topics/depression.html
http://depression.about.com/
www.depression.com/

---

*The authors of this book cannot guarantee that all content in these resources will conform
to biblical teaching or affirm the information presented in *Seeing in the Dark*. They are
included here as resources for further information only; their inclusion does not imply
endorsement by the authors or publisher.

Endnotes

chapter 1

1. www.timelessquotes.com/author/Dr._R._W._Shepherd.html.
2. W. Katon and H. Schulberg, "Epidemiology of Depression in Primary Care," *Gen Hosp Psychiatry* 14 (1992): 237.
3. "Treatment of Major Depression," *Agency for Health Care Policy and Research* 93–0551 (1993).
4. R. M. Crum, L. Cooper-Patrick, and D. E. Ford, "Depressive Symptoms Among General Medical Patients: Prevalence and one-year outcome," *Psychosom Med* 56 (1994): 109.
5. J. L. Jackson, P. G. O'Malley, and K. Kroenke, "Clinical Predictors of Mental Disorders Among Medical Outpatients," *Psychosomatics* 39 (1998): 431.
6. G. E. Simon, M. VonKorff, and M. Piccinelli, et al., "An International Study of the Relation Between Somatic Symptoms and Depression," *N Engl J Med* 341 (1999): 1329.
7. U. Halbreich and L. A. Lumley, "The Multiple Interactional Biological Processes That Might Lead to Depression and Gender Differences in Its Appearance," *J Affect Disord* 29 (1993): 159.
8. American Psychiatric Association, *Diagnostic and Statistical Manual of Mental Disorders,* 4th ed (DSM-IV-PC) (1995).
9. S. M. Stahl, "Basic Psychopharmacology of Antidepressants, Part 1: Antidepressants have seven distinct mechanisms of action," *J Clin Psychiatry (Suppl 4)* 59 (1998): 5.
10. F. E. Bloom and D. J. Kupfer, eds., *Psychopharmacology: The Fourth Generation of Progress* (New York: Raven Press, 1995), 933.
11. American Psychiatric Association, "Practice Guideline for the Treatment of Patient With Major Depressive Disorder," *Am J Psychiatry (Suppl 4)* 157 (2000): 1.
12. P. Videbech and B. Ravnkilde, "Hippocampal Volume and Depression: A meta-analysis of MRI studies," *Am J Psychiatry* 161 (2004): 1957.

chapter 2

1. "A TIA is a 'warning stroke' or 'mini-stroke' that produces stroke-like symptoms but does no lasting damage. Recognizing and treating TIAs can reduce your risk of a major stroke. . . . TIAs occur when a blood clot temporarily clogs an artery, and part of the brain doesn't get the blood it needs. The symptoms occur rapidly and last a relatively short time. Most TIAs last less than five minutes. The average is about a minute. Unlike a stroke, when a TIA is over, there's no injury to the brain" (*www.americanheart.org/presenter.jhtml?identifier=4781*).
2. Aspirin is not trivial for TIAs. It can be life-saving.
3. "Shields, Osmond Conclude: This Guy's from Mars," *Arizona Republic,* July 2, 2005, *azcentral.com.*
4. Focus on the Family study (1998), cited on *www.pastorsincovenant.org/ clergyfact.htm* (accessed April 11, 2006).
5. E. Glen Wagner, "Walking Alone," *Rev!* magazine (May/June 2005): 50.
6. In his modesty, Phil would argue with this statement, but a church with over one thousand attending (many of whom are new Christians), in one of the most affluent communities in the United States, is a remarkable achievement.
7. I (Rich) feel that Phil is, perhaps, describing people who have been heavily medicated for schizophrenia.
8. Satinder Bindra, "Mother Teresa's Letters Reveal Doubts," September 7, 2001, *cnn.com.*
9. Frank Lattimore, "Mother Teresa, Daughter of God?" *members.aol.com/tlbministries/MotherTeresa.html.*

chapter 3

1. Gary Kinnaman, *My Companion Through Grief* (Ventura, CA: Regal Books, 2004).
2. M. B. First, ed., *Diagnostic and Statistical Manual of Mental Disorder,* 4th ed. (Washington, D.C.: American Psychiatric Association, 1994).
3. J. Wang and S. B. Patten, "The Moderating Effects of Coping Strategies on Major Depression in the General Population," *Can J Psychiatry* 47, no. 2 (2002): 167–73; P. J. O'Connor, N. P. Pronk, A. Tan, et al., "Characteristics of Adults Who Use Prayer As an Alternative Therapy," *Am J Health Promot* 19, no. 5 (2005): 369–75; J. Tloczynski and S.

Fritzsch, "Intercessory Prayer in Psychological Well-Being: Using a multiple-baseline, across-subjects design," *Psychol Rep* 91, no. 3 (2002): 731–41.

4. R. C. Kessler, K. A. McGonagle, S. Zhao, et al., "Lifetime and 12-Month Prevalence of DSM-III-R Psychiatric Disorders in the United States," *Arch Gen Psychiatry* 51, no. 1 (1994): 8–19; G. E. Simon, E. J. Ludman, S. Tutty, et al., "Telephone Psychotherapy and Telephone Care Management for Primary Care Patients Starting Antidepressant Treatment: A randomized controlled trial," *JAMA* 292, no. 8 (2004): 935–42.

5. W. Katon, P. Robinson, M. Von Korff, et al., "A Multifaceted Intervention to Improve Treatment of Depression in Primary Care," *Arch Gen Psychiatry* 53, no. 10 (1996): 924–32.

chapter 4

1. M. Nobile, G. M. Cataldo, C. Marino, et al., "Diagnosis and Treatment of Dysthymia in Children and Adolescents," *CNS Drugs* 17, no. 13 (2003): 927–46.

2. M. Silva de Lima and M. Hotopf, "A Comparison of Active Drugs for the Treatment of Dysthymia," *Cochrane Database Syst Rev* CD-ROM, 2003.

3. M. F. de Mello, L. M. Myczcowisk, and P. R. Menezes, "A Randomized Controlled Trial Comparing Moclobemide and Moclobemide Plus Interpersonal Psychotherapy in the Treatment of Dysthymic Disorder," *J Psychother Pract Res* 10, no. 2 (2001): 117–23.

4. J. B. Potash and J. R. DePaulo Jr., "Searching High and Low: A review of the genetics of bipolar disorder," *Bipolar Disord* 2, no. 1 (2000): 8–26.

5. T. Suppes, E. B. Dennehy, and E. W. Gibbons, "The Longitudinal Course of Bipolar Disorder," *J Clin Psychiatry* 61, Suppl. 9 (2000): 23–30.

6. S. C. Dilsaver and S. Henderson-Fuller, "Occult Mood Disorders in 104 Consecutively Presenting Children Referred for the Treatment of Attention-Deficit/Hyperactivity Disorder in a Community Mental Health Clinic," *J Clin Psychiatry* 64, no. 10 (2003): 1170–6.

7. Lithium carbonate is very helpful in controlling and preventing mania. Anticonvulsant medicines, like carbamazepine (Tegretol), can also

stabilize mood [P. E. Keck Jr. and S. L. McElroy, "Outcome in the Pharmacologic Treatment of Bipolar Disorder," *J Clin Psychopharmacol* 16, Suppl 2 (1996): 15S–23S.] Traditional antidepressant medications are prescribed when depression is a prominent feature in the patient's clinical picture.

8. "Practice Guideline for the Treatment of Patients With Bipolar Disorder," *Am J Psychiatry* 151 (1994): 1.

9. T. Partonen and J. Lonnqvist, "Seasonal Affective Disorder," *Lancet* 352, no. 9137 (1998): 1369–74.

10. L. Sher, "Genetic Studies of Seasonal Affective Disorder and Seasonality," *Compr Psychiatry* 42, no. 2 (2001): 105–10.

11. S. A. Checkley, D. G. Murphy, M. Abbas, et al., "Melatonin Rhythms in Seasonal Affective Disorder," *Br J Psychiatry* 163 (1993): 332–7.

12. V. Coiro, R. Volpi, C. Marchesi, et al., "Abnormal Serotonergic Control of Prolactin and Cortisol Secretion in Patients With Seasonal Affective Disorder," *Psychoneuroendocrinology* 18, no. 8 (1993): 551–6.

13. R. N. Golden, B. N. Gaynes, R. D. Ekstrom, et al., "The Efficacy of Light Therapy in the Treatment of Mood Disorders: A review and meta-analysis of the evidence," *Am J Psychiatry* 162, no. 4 (2005): 656–62.

14. A. Neumeister, E. H. Turne, J. R. Matthews, et al., "Effects of Tryptophan Depletion vs. Catecholamine Depletion in Patients With Seasonal Affective Disorder in Remission With Light Therapy," *Arch Gen Psychiatry* 55, no. 6 (1998): 524–30.

15. D. H. Avery, D. N. Eder, M. A. Bolte, et al., "Dawn Simulation and Bright Light in the Treatment of SAD: A controlled study," *Biol Psychiatry* 50, no. 3 (2001): 250–16.

16. World Entertainment News Network, "Cruise Slams Shields' Drug Use," Wed. May 25, 2005. *www.hollywood.com/news/detail/id/2440860*.

17. *Arizona Republic* (July 2, 2005).

18. *Entertainment Weekly* (June 17, 2005): 29.

19. *Diagnostic and Statistical Manual of Mental Disorders,* 4th ed. (Washington, D.C.: American Psychiatric Association, 1994).

20. A. Whitton, R. Warner, and L. Appleby, "The Pathway to Care in Post-Natal Depression: Women's attitudes to post-natal depression and its treatment," *Br J Gen Pract* 46, no. 408 (1996): 427–8.

21. J. Evans, J. Heron, H. Francomb, et al., "Cohort Study of Depressed

Mood During Pregnancy and After Childbirth," *BMJ* 323, no. 7307 (2001): 257–60.

22. M. Steiner, "Postpartum Psychiatric Disorders," *Can J Psychiatry* 35, no. 1 (1990): 89–95.

23. M. W. O'Hara, J. A. Schlecht, D. A. Lewis, et al., "Prospective Study of Postpartum Blues: Biologic and psychosocial factors," *Arch Gen Psychiatry* 48, no. 9 (1991): 801–6.

24. M. Bloch, P. J. Schmidt, M. Danaceau, et al., "Effects of Gonadal Steroids in Women With a History of Postpartum Depression," *Am J Psychiatry* 157, no. 6 (2000): 924–30.

25. I. M. Terp and P. B. Mortensen, "Postpartum Psychoses: Clinical diagnoses and relative risk of admission after parturition," *Br J Psychiatry* 172 (1998): 521–6.

26. R. E. Kendell, J. C. Chalmers, and C. Platz, "Epidemiology of Puerperal Psychoses," *Br J Psychiatry* 150 (1987): 662–73.

27. C. M. Klier, M. Muzik. K. L. Rosenblum, et al., Interpersonal psychotherapy adapted for the group setting in the treatment of postpartum depression. *J Psychother Pract Res* (Spring 2001): 10, no. 2: 124–31.

chapter 5

1. Steven D. Passik, PhD; Margaret V. McDonald, MSW; William M. Dugan Jr., MD, et al., "Depression in Cancer Patients" *Medscape Psychiatry & Mental Health eJournal* 2, no. 3, 1997.

2. D. D. Dunlop, L. S. Lyons, L. M. Manheim, et al., *Med Care* 42, no. 6 (2004): 502–11.

3. E. Shortall, D. Isenber, and S. P. Newman, "Factors Associated With Mood and Mood Disorders in SLE," *Lupus* 4, no. 4 (1995): 272–9.

4. T. Covic, B. Adamson, D. Spencer, et al., *Rheumatology* 42, no. 11 (2003): 1287–94.

5. B. Malzberg, "Mortality Among Patients With Involution Melancholia," *Am J Psychiatry* 93 (1937): 1231.

6. J. J. Miguel-Hidalgo and G. Rakowska, "Morphologic Brain Changes in Depression: Can antidepressants reverse them?" *CNS Drugs* 16, no. 6 (2002): 361–72.

7. H. K. Meier-Ewert, P. M. Ridker, N. Rifai, et al., "Effect of Sleep Loss on C-Reactive Protein, an Inflammatory Marker of Cardiovascular Risk," *J Am Coll Cardiol* 43, no. 4 (2004): 676–83.

8. T. Lange, B. Perras, H. L. Fehm, et al., "Sleep Enhances the Human Antibody Response to Hepatitis A Vaccination," *Psychosom Mad* 65, no. 5 (2003): 831–5.

9. A. Schuld, M. Haack, D. Hinze-Seich, et al., "Experimental Studies on the Interaction Between Sleep and the Immune System in Humans," *Psychother Psychosom Med Psychol* 55, no. 1 (2005): 29–35.

10. D. Riemann, M. Berger, and U. Voderholzer, "Sleep and Depression— Results From Psychobiological Studies: An Overview," *Biol Psychol* 57, nos. 1–3 (2001): 67–103.

11. J. A. Gall and G. M. Edelman, "Neural Reapportionment: An hypothesis to account for the function of sleep," *C R Biol* 327, no. 8 (2004): 721–7; R. Lechin, B. Pardy-Maldonado, B. van der Dijs, et al., "Circulating Neurotransmitters During the Different Wake-Sleep Stages in Normal Subjects," *Psychoneuroendocrinology* 29, no. 5 (2004): 669–85.

12. A. Wirz-Justice and R. H. Van den Hoofsdakker, "Sleep Deprivation in Depression: What do we know, where do we go?" *Biol Psychiatry* 46, no. 4 (1999): 445–53.

13. D. F. Kripke, "Light Treatment of Non-Seasonal Depression: Speed, efficacy, and combined treatment," *J Affect Disord* 49, no. 2 (1998): 109–17.

14. S. Leppamaki, T. Partonen, and J. Lonnqvist, "Bright-Light Exposure Combined With Physical Exercise Elevates Mood," *J Affect Disord* 72, no. 2 (2002): 139–44.

15. B. Nemets, S. Ziva, and R. Belmaker, "Addition of Omega–3 Fatty Acid to Maintenance Medication Treatment for Recurrent Unipolar Depressive Disorder," *Am J Psychiatry* 159 (2002): 477–479.

16. FDA Communication, 1994.

17. R. G. Walton, R. Hudak, and R. Green-Waite, "Adverse Reactions to Aspartame: Double-blind challenge in patients from a vulnerable population," *Biol Psychiatry* 34 (1993): 13–17.

18. Good Housekeeping Institute, "New Good Housekeeping Institute study finds drastic discrepancy in potencies of popular herbal supplement," news release, March 3, 1998.

19. Monmaney T. Labels' potency claims often inaccurate, analysis finds. Spot check of products finds widely varying levels of key ingredient. But some firms object to testing method and defend their brands' quality. *Los Angeles Times*, Aug 31, 1998.

20. Hypericum Depression Trial Study Group, "Effect of Hypericum perforatum (Saint-John's-wort) in major depressive disorder," *JAMA* 287 (2002): 1807–14.
21. S. C. Piscitelli et al., "Indinavir Concentrations and Saint-John's-wort," *Lancet* 355 (2000): 547.
22. K. A. Jobst, et al., "Safety of Saint-John's-wort," *Lancet* 355 (2000): 576.
23. The Medical Letter 39: 107–108, 1997.
24. Thomas Kramer, MD, "Transcranial Magnetic Stimulation and Its Effectiveness in Affective Disorders," Medscape Internet *www.medscape.com/viewarticle/420840*.

chapter 6

1. Larry Crabb, *Effective Biblical Counseling* (Grand Rapids, MI: Zondervan Publishing, 1977), 61–73.
2. D. J. Rumford, *Soul Shaping* (Wheaton, IL: Tyndale House Publishers, Inc., 1996), 12–15.
3. Strong's Concordance Word Number 5060.
4. S. Ventegodt, M. Morad, J. Merrick, "Clinical Holistic Medicine: Classic Art of Healing or Therapeutic Touch," *Scientific World Journal* 4 (2004): 134–47.

chapter 7

1. Charles Hodge, "Commentary on the Second Epistle to the Corinthians," QuickVerse, 2003.
2. Colin Allen, "Type A: Hard on the Heart," October 23, 2003. *www.psychologytoday.com*.
3. Richard Francis Weymouth, *The New Testament in Modern Speech* (London: James Clarke and Co., 1903), n.p.
4. The statement "The Lord is near" refers to the second coming of Christ, that His return is near. I'm drawing an application that the Lord is near us all the time, as Jesus said, "The kingdom of God is within you," and "The kingdom of God is near."

chapter 8

1. Horst Balz and Gerhard Schneider, eds., *The Exegetical Dictionary of the New Testament*, vol. 2 (Grand Rapids: Eerdman's, 1991), 417.

2. Tim Stafford, "Where Stormie Finds Her Power," *Christianity Today* (July 2004): 44.
3. Ibid.

chapter 9

1. Eva Bender, "Brain Data Reveal Why Psychotherapy Works," *Psychiatric News* (May 7, 2004): 34. This article begins: "Mounting evidence on psychotherapy shows that it is effective and can even alter the brain's chemistry." This was the message delivered by researchers and educators at the daylong seminar "Scholarly Activity in Psychotherapy Training," which was held in conjunction with the annual meeting of the American Association of Directors of Psychiatric Residency Training (AADPRT) in New Orleans in March. . . . For those with psychiatric illnesses, the "experiential learning" from cognitive-behavioral therapy (CBT) has been shown to alter some of the same biological mechanisms typically affected by medications.
2. *www.cutechoice.com/cgi-bin/create/author.pl?auth=Thomas_Szasz*
3. Gary Kinnaman and Alfred Ells, *Leaders That Last: How Covenant Friendships Can Help Pastors Thrive* (Grand Rapids: Baker Books, 2003).
4. B. A. Amow, M. J. Constantino, "Effectiveness of Psychotheraphy and Combination Treatment for Chronic Depression," *Journal of Clinical Psychology* 59 (2003): 893–905.
5. Joshua Wolf Shenk, "Lincoln's Great Depression," *Atlantic* (September 2005): 66.

chapter 10

1. A portion of this chapter is a revision of chapter 7 in my (Gary's) book, *Dumb Things Smart Christians Believe* (Grand Rapids: Servant/Vine), 1999. Unfortunately, this book is currently out of print. Used copies may be available at amazon.com or other Web sites.
2. Dwight Carlson, "Exposing the Myth That Christians Should Not Have Emotional Problems," *Christianity Today,* February 3, 1998, 30.
3. Ibid.
4. "Living With Depression: Caly's Story," *health.ivillage.com,* n.d.
5. Brennan Manning, *The Wisdom of Accepted Tenderness* (Rockaway, NJ: Dimension Books, 1983), n.p.

Scripture Index

Index of Medications

Subject Index